Inka Mountain Magic

By: Zane Curfman

Undomesticated books

ISBN-13:
978-1463503307

ISBN-10:
146350330X

Table of Contents

Introduction

I invite you to accompany me on a journey of spiritual discovery and growth -a journey that took me into the roots of Inkan spirituality and healing. This journey involves a living tradition that started well before the rise of the Inka. It dates back over 1600 years, to the first peoples of South America.

Like all peoples of the Andes, the Inka had a preoccupation with living spiritual energies. These ancient seers knew there was no separation between the sacred and mundane; all things were manifestations of spiritual energy.

Much of this ancient way of life has been preserved by a group of Indians: the Q-ero (K*'ero*), who live high in the mountains above Cusco, Peru. The Q'ero are considered the keepers of ancient spiritual ways. They have preserved one of the most ancient forms of Andean spirituality. This "Living Tradition" has been passed from Grandparent-to-Grandchild since before written history.

Isolated high in the mountains, the Q'ero lived, for the most part, unnoticed. Then, Spanish land owners took over some of the indigenous people's ancestral lands. The Q'ero, being a passive, gentle people, were easily led into a type of slavery called, "The Haciendado System."

In 1949, a team of fifteen anthropologists, led by Oscar Nunez del Prado, mounted the first Expedition to Q'ero's. Oscar, with the help of: Emiliano Waman T'ika, Demetrio Tupac Yupanqui, and Mario Vasquez -started the legal, labor, and reform movements. This led to the Q'ero actually buying back their lands, and to the establishment of the Q'ero Nations, in 1958.

My first teacher and initiator to the path, was Juan Nunez del Prado, Oscar's son. I have also worked in-depth with my good friend and sister on the path, Elizabeth Jenkins. I have had the great fortune to visit and live with the Q'ero, and to experience the tradition first-hand. I have worked with my friends, the Q'ero masters: Don Marcos Q'espi, Don Alipo Q'espi, Don Modesto Q'espi Lonasqo, and Don Fermin Flores.

This path has changed my life, allowing me to commune with spirit and feel the touch of God. This is not a rare or supernatural occurrence. It is everyone's birth-right, and is as natural as taking a breath, childbirth, or a good meal.

This book will present the practical working of this wisdom to the modern mind. The path of the "Paqo Kuna" (pronounced *pah-ko* which means, "nature mystic" and koon-a which means "people"), is not a secret society or mystery school. Complicated philosophy and metaphysical formulae are not a part of this tradition. It is open to everyone, regardless of religion or cultural background. It is introspection into our daily walk; its laboratory is life. The teachings have been passed down from the primal, and refined through generations of practice. This makes the knowledge practical, workable, and open to all who seek.

The teachings in this book come from the Kurak Akulleq (*kur-ack ak-cool-ick*) -a very rare branch of the

Alto Misayoq (*mes-i-yoak*) path. In the end, it will not be this book that teaches you, but your own experience. This is a personal path based on your perceptions. It is an art, because it is the personal expression and application of your perceptions. With practice, you can become better at it. With this material, I strive to present the tradition of the Q'ero, as has been taught to me by both my Q'ero and Mestizo teachers. This book is intended to present the tradition in a way that all people can understand, making this simple wisdom workable in your daily life.

One of the goals of every spiritual tradition is the harmonious life of the community, and the growth of the individual in that community. In the end, we need each other. None of us grow or achieve anything on our own. We are all supported by a family of spirits, the land we live and walk on, the nature beings that watch over us, the Holy One that enlightens us and the Earth that provides for us. We are also empowered by the bones, wisdom, and love of the ancestors, through which we build our stairways to heaven.

Salud, Pachamama! Salud, Wiraqocha! Salud, Apus and Nustas! Salud, Q'ero!

Chapter <u>1</u>
Dance of the Rainbow

It was April of 2003, when I found myself on the verge of fulfilling a life-long dream. From early on, I knew I had the power to create change. I could make others feel better. I also had a capacity to "just know" things. I never really saw it as helping others though, but as play, and I loved to play and see what resulted. I learned how to play with others to make them feel better; I also knew how to play with others and make them feel worse. I was sensitive enough that I always knew how best to push someone's buttons.

I am about an eighth Cree Indian, and a mix of other unknown native lines. Unfortunately, the roots to our tribe had been purposefully destroyed and hidden. I have known most my life, that I was a medicine man.

This is to say, that I could not go to my family, or tribe, for instruction.

My father was a very spiritual man; he was a Baptist preacher and a Freemason. My mother is blessed in this life with a psychic gift. However, since she is a Christian, she always thought it wrong to use this gift and never developed it. I knew from early on, that I was not a Christian; I hated church and the masks people would wear there. It seemed less about a one-on-one experience with the divine, and more about an indoctrination of rules to follow.

Now, I found myself winding up snow-covered interstates during a torrential blizzard. It was April, and my best friends, Megan and Josh, were escorting me to a meeting with my new teacher, Juan Victor Nunez del Prado. Juan was teaching a group of us how to give the Hatun Karpay, or "Great Initiation", using the sacred landscapes of North America. As we were crossing from New York to Connecticut, the snow started falling. In fifteen minutes, there was more than a foot on the roads. We could not believe how people where driving. People were passing us left and right: trucks, cars, and semis. Predictably, we would soon pass the same vehicles, now motionless, wrecked, and piled-up in the median. It was, truly, terror inspiring -watching Semis beside us loose control and start jack-knifing and sliding all over the interstate.

I had discovered Juan through a series of interesting coincidences. I have been involved in spiritualism and energy-work all of my life. It was something very natural to me. Off-and-on through my youth, I would devote myself to learning more of these mystical arts, which came so naturally. The downside of being a natural is: I knew that I had the ability to do these things, but I did not have the capacity to use these abilities at-will. By the time I was a senior in high school, I felt I had learned all there was to learn of the mystical side of things.

The fire was rekindled in me at age 23, when after having ingested a poison, I was convulsing violently. My best-friend, Megan, was with me. She sat down behind me, and placed her hands on my head. Instantly, I felt this flow of relieving energy. I somehow knew the energy, but could not understand how she had

the ability to turn it on at-will. She told me it was
something she had learned from a man named, Ed
Shin. Ed had lived in Tibet for many years and worked
with the shamans there. I came to find out it was a mix
of Raku Ki Reiki, and the ancient shamanic practices of
Tibet. I asked her to teach me. She said she would, but
had not finished her training yet. Two years later,
Megan, Josh (my other best-friend), and I found a Reiki
Master: the Rev. Jason Storm. Soon after, we all
became Reiki Masters. We started to channel some
interesting symbols. I started to have visions of these
little, stone huts with flags. As we worked more with
these new energies, we realized that we were
connecting with an intelligence. It was a rainbow
serpent. It told us it would teach us to heal, help make
the earth green again, and prepare us for our next step
in our spiritual path. We named her Tolsie, after a
person in the Hindu tradition (Tulsi). Tulsi, through her
devotion to Lord Krishna, was made into a sacred tree
whose wood is used to make the malas that mantras
(sacred chants) are counted on.

I started to look up the things Tolsie was teaching on the Internet -to see if anyone else was using them. I found a group of Indians, in Peru, that were working with the living energies in much the same way. A few names kept popping up. I was drawn to Juan. Then I saw a picture of him. I was blown away! I had seen this exact image before in a vision of a spiritual guide. The picture was of a bald man, dressed in all white, with a little beard, sitting on a rock. It was an identical image. Another interesting coincidence happened when I was talking to Juan for the first time. He told me he came on this trip to work with the rainbow energies. I was astounded. I told him of our experience while channeling in a Reiki circle, and showed him the master symbol that came to us while working with Tolsie. I drew it in the dust; he smiled, and told me this was the energy he had come to North America to receive/work with.

Juan and I at Shelburne Falls Massachusetts 2003.

Chapter 2

The Prophecy of the Inka

Juan Nunez del Prado has spent much of his academic and spiritual life collecting, recording, and piecing together bits of the Inkan prophesy. He found that of all the people he interviewed, it was two paqos: the esteemed Dons Benito Qoriwaman and Andres Espinosa, that held the totality of the prophesy. Don Benito and Don Andres did not pass the knowledge of this prophesy on to their Q'ero students. The last generation of Q'ero's seemed to all hold some general knowledge of it. In my time spent with the Q'ero's, I found no one in this current generation that has much, if any, knowledge of it.

I believe the prophecy was passed down, just not in the rigid, literal way we (Westerners) view prophesy.

The Q'ero are a practical people. Certain practical parts of the prophecy are universally known, like the understanding of the Pachakuti (*pah-cha-coo-ti*), which are predictable cycles of space/time that mark the end and beginning of an age. Also, there is the idea that the Inkari, or the First Inka, is still alive, and one day will return. There is the concept of Yanatin -harmonious relationships based on differences, and the "Teripaypacha" -the time of meeting ourselves again.

There is also the process of Katarismo which we will discuss in some detail in a bit. I think my friend and teacher, Don Modesto, said it best: "Yes, I have heard many prophecies. Every Paqo has a prophecy. It doesn't matter; what is important is that 'we', the threads, are weaving back together now."

In the west, we see prophecy as something very rigid. It must be understood that the prophetic traditions of the native peoples, of all the Americas, are more ambiguous. We could see them as "What if?" prophecies. You see, prophecy is a tool to help get us where were going in our lives. Prophecy is a map, not a destination. It is based in the Lloque (*low-key*) art of divination.

When we divine for someone, we are with the help of the Apus (*ah-poos*/mountain spirits), and often with the aid of coca, taking an assessment of the state of that person's energy. With the help of the Apus, we can flow forward on the wave of Kausay (*cow-say*/living energy) to see what is possible for them at their current energy-state. Which wave of Kausay is flowing towards their highest good? What things may be blocking the way? We also find out how we can best help the person arrive at that place. Alberto Villoldo calls this, "Destiny Retrieval". This does not mean it is the only possible outcome. We are looking at many possible outcomes. We are finding which wave is best for them to ride, and how to help them do this. So be it with prophecy: it was an assessment of where we were as humans, and what possible places we could go from that place (including things that will help us get there).

The Pachacuti Prophecy is best to be looked at as an engineered opportunity. There are three major aspects to the prophecy: The Pachacuti ("World Turned Upside Down"), the Teripay Pacha ("Age of Meeting Ourselves"), and the arrival of a new type of human consciousness.

World Turned Upside Down

Many people relate the Pachacuti with the Mayan prophecy of 2012, the Hopi's emergence of the 5th world, and the Christian Apocalypse. Though there are some interesting similarities, they are not interchangeable with each other.

The Pachacuti already happened. It began Aug 1st of 1991, and lasted to Aug 1st of 1993. Looking back at that time period, there was a fundamental change in reality. At that time, society seemed to be shifting to honor more individualism, actualization, and community. This is said to be a possible taste of the coming age. I say possible, because it is in our hands to decide where we are going. This prophecy, like all prophecy, is meant to be used as a guide. The Seers of the ancient world took an assessment of humanity, our gifts, and already expressed potential; they followed our collective flows of living energy into the future. Based on what they discovered, they created myths, legends, rituals, codes and ethics that would remind/encode into us our greatest potentials. These Seers put into action a program of social engineering, leading us towards who we are becoming. We are now at a point in time-space where their vision ends.

Now, we are in our own hands. The myths and legends of the past led us here, and now you and I must take the lead. The myths and legends of the past will no longer have the power to influence our children. The ways in which we live our lives will become the myths and legends of the future! Be yourself, and follow your heart!

Age of Meeting Ourselves

The time period from 1993 on, is called the Teripaypacha or, "Age of Meeting Ourselves". During this time, all things will return to their natural state. This is a time that has the potential to be very violent, depending on how well we accept ourselves. During the Teripaypacha, a type of cosmic tupay (fight, or challenge) is occurring as the, "old energies" (qualities like community, equality, and acceptance emerge. As this happens, the "new energies" (the modern ways of life based on ego-centered, hegemonic world view) fight to regain control.

In the Andes, the communal qualities are symbolized as a serpent. The newer, egocentric ways of life are symbolized as a conquering lion.

There are only two outcomes from tupay:

1. Kuti (to turn upside down) - These energies can be seen as two waves heading towards each other. As they clash (tupay), a wall is built. The

wall continues to grow, until the side with more energies and direction behind it, caps the wall and spills over the other side (as the wall crashes to the ground in oppression).

2. Taqe (harmony) - Using the same wave model as used in the first example: the two energies rush at each other and clash, but as the wall is being built the two waves find some similarity in each other. Places where they are equal (masi), start to flow through each other (taqe), and become harmonious with each other -accepting each other's similarities and differences. This is Yannatin, harmonious relationships between the differences. Yanantin come from knowing how you are like each other, and embracing each other for these likenesses. It involves seeing how we are different, and adoring each other for these differences.

During this time, the living grids of the universe are in alignment with self-exploration. This plays out in the psyche of humanity between the "Superego"(all that one wants to be), and the "Shadow" (all that someone does not want to accept within themselves). Part of knowing the self, is learning about your individual heritage and finding pride and love for your genetic past.

The Four Tribes of Man

Re-meeting ourselves functions beyond the personal scope, into the genetic and universal plane. All of the ancient spiritual traditions of the world recount, roughly, the same story.

Though the details from tradition-to-tradition differ, the ancient wisdom describes there are originally four tribes of man. Each tribe was like a personification of the four basic elements: the black tribe, water; the red tribe, earth; the white tribe, fire; and the yellow tribe, air. Through these elements, each tribe understood and communicated with the natural and spiritual worlds. Each tribe was called by the spirits of lands, where they could grow the most and explore their own individuality. One day, they parted to explore the world, knowing that eventually they would meet again and share all they had learned -becoming one people. We are living in this time now.

Part of the work to be done in this age is finding respect for your genetic past and healing ancestral lines.

Healing these family lines allows us to receive an uncorrupted flow of energies from our ancestors. The idea is: you have to know where you have been, before you know where you are going. All family lines hold certain spiritual gifts. Every race and culture holds essential wisdom needed for the evolution of humanity. It is perhaps more important at this time, than any before, that each of us reclaim our ancestral knowledge and share it with each other for the good of all.

An interesting note: it is not through how we are all alike that we will grow and evolve, but through honoring how we are different. In fact, these difficult, uncomfortable differences between us are where the real gold of existence hides. In other words, differences are the catalyst of alchemical change.

As each one of us, learns to respect our ancestors and the gifts of our families, we gain a type of self esteem. By seeing family quarks and uniqueness as gifts destined to help all humanity, we also gain the ability to accept where others come from as gifts of perception.

The Teripay pacha is not only a time of re-meeting ourselves in a genetic and cultural ways, but of also re-meeting (and starting a dialog with) our fellow creation. Through deliberate acknowledgment, and interaction with spirits and nature beings, we start to reunite the seen and unseen worlds. In this way, through our combined efforts, we can usher in the Golden Age of the Taripay Pacha.

Emergence of a New Human

We are, at this time, awaiting the arrival of a new type of human consciousness. As more and more people around the world awaken into the fourth level of psycho-spiritual consciousness, or the understanding that all is sacred and a living miracle, we create a type of womb of possibility. Any of us may emerge from this womb with this new level of psycho-spiritual development. According to the Prophecy, this will first accrue at the Q'ori rit'y Festival in Peru. Q'ori rit'y is the festival of the divine masculine. Consequently, the first will be male. The male of the fifth level is called, in Quechua, Inka Mallku. A female of the fifth level is called Inka Nusta.

This first Mallku will travel along the seqes, ancient lines of energy, connecting wakas/sacred sites toward Cuzco. At this same moment, another Mallku will appear, near the Wiraqocha temple, in Raqchi. He will also follow the seqes to Cuzco, where the two Mallkus will meet at the festival of Corpus Christi.

Simultaneously, the third Mallku, will manifest at the shrine of Taytacha Temblores, in Cuzco, where the three Mallkus unite.

Together, the Mallkus will travel to Lima, where they will meet the fourth Mallku, and first Nusta, at either the sanctuary of Nazarenas, or the sanctuary of Pachakamilla.

This group of paqos will then travel by boat to the south of Peru. There, at the Sanctuary of the Virgin of Chapi, in Arequipa, the group will meet the second Nusta. This group then travels to Bolivia, where the third Nusta will reveal herself at the Sanctuary of the Virgin of Copacabana. Then, they travel to Puno, where they meet the fourth Nusta at the Sanctuary of the Virgin of Cadelaria.

Returning to Wiraqocha temple in Cuzco, the Mallku and Nusta must await the arrival of the last pair of fifth level paqos, two Mallku and two Nusta -whom will come from the North.

This "Fifth Level" comes with certain spiritual attributes. One is the ability to heal any illness with a touch of the hand, and nothing more. No flowing of energy, no prayer, no holding of sacred space, not even intent, just the healing of everything, every-time, with a simple touch.

Another attribute of the Inka Mallku, is the ability to travel through holes in time.

If this sounds hard to believe, look into any of the world's spiritual traditions, and you will find legends and tales of this very thing. You see, the Inka Mallku is not really a new level of consciousness. There have always been individuals who have attained it from direct spiritual communion. What is new is that, in this age, it will spread also by the touch of the hand.

Once all twelve Mallku and Nustas are united at the Temple of Wiraqocha, together they will create the energy field necessary by playing out the ritual crowning ceremony of the Inka. This is to birth the first male/female couple of the sixth level of psycho-spiritual development. It is not known if this sixth level couple will emerge from the twelve gathered, or if it will be somebody else.

The Return of the Inka

This spiritually enlightened couple of the sixth level, is known in Quechua as the "Sapa Inka" (sole lord), and the feminine is the Qoya. They will be recognized by a type of light that surrounds their bodies. Together, they will Travel to Cuzco, where they will reestablish, and awaken the new Inka Empire.

The name of the Inkan Empire was, Tawantinsuyu, meaning "the country or land of the four corners". Many Paqos myself included; believe the four corners of the new Tawantinsuyu symbolize the uniting of the four tribes of man, the acceptance of our differences as divine, and the open exchange of ideas.

From the new dawn of the Tawantinsuyu, the Sapa Inka and Qoya will serve as models for political leaders everywhere -teaching them to lead with love and respect, and teaching all how to live in harmony with nature. This will usher in the reinfusion of the world with light -leading to the golden age of the Taripay Pacha, when the metaphysical city of Paytiti reappears.

This is where the first Inka has been waiting, and will manifest, reuniting with his children. The three worlds will merge, (upper, middle, and lower) forming a new world.

Katarismo

Flowing throughout the prophecy of the Pachcuti and the Taripaypacha, are the symbols and living energies of Katarismo. This is not to be confused with the democratic political movement, started in the 1970's, of the same name. Nor, is it to be confused with rebellious uprisings of the Aymara Chief, Tomas Katari, or Tupac Amaru II. Though all of these movements hold, at their heart, key ideas and philosophies found in the Aboriginal Katarismo. The name, Katari, comes from the Quechua word, "Qallari" meaning to start or begin.

The original, fundamental ray of the universe looked like a serpent with flaming wings. As it went about creating the cosmos, it created in its own image. First it made the stars, then all the planets within the Milky Way. When the ray came to Earth, it was in the form of a fire serpent, with wings of rainbow colors. Upon landing, it became an egg shaped stone, then a serpent. This constituted the principle of all life — expressing the force and origin of fertility.

Mother Earth is fertilized through the serpentine rays of Father Sun, which are like semen fertilizing and bringing fourth her children (all the rocks, plants, animals, and humans). Mother Earth feeds her children from mountains, which are her breasts, from which serpentine streams and rivers spring.

The Katari movement, basically, is a movement to restore the similitude of the creator into the human-population-serpent. This offers us a guide to achieving personal and global freedom. As a metaphor, it expresses the need to know ourselves, and to have pride for who we are as humans —healing our ancestry, and finding respect for our forbearers. It also infers how this is not possible on a personal level, without first activating our seed of personal power. This requires for germination a re-establishment of interpersonal relationships with nature.

This reconnection is not based in the rules of ecology, but on the realization that the Earth is a living being, more then that, she is our authentic mother. When we quiet ourselves in nature, we naturally start to blend our essence with that of the local nature beings. Thus, we learn to engage in the spiritual language of energy. This is a new language ¬not a metaphor. Nature can speak with us and help us to learn about ourselves ¬our abilities. This is not a one- way street, though, it is a friendship. It is a kinship with the natural world, and all relations are based on reciprocity, mutual respect, and love.

The nature beings and the Earth, soften us, opening us to their wisdom and awakening our seed of personal power ¬the very similitude of the Creator. This re-establishes our ability to recognize the sacred in the natural world (and within ourselves). Then, we each become like the Katari: a ray of unique light, pinning into the Earth, a feather. The Amru (great serpent without wings) is part of this prophesy. When enough people of the world have awakened into similitude and join together, they will spread, throughout humanity, the laws of the Pacha (respect for nature). Also, the Ideals of: unity, acceptance, tolerance, equality, and the complementary nature of differences (seeing our differences as individual uniqueness and something in which to be proud) will be disseminated. As these ideals spread, it announces the abandonment of our current egocentric, fear-based ideology. It will help us remember we are all one family (symbolically creating rainbow colored wings). This movement of unity builds, leading to the birth of a new multi-national Tawatinsuyu ("Empire of the Four Corners"). Instead of a single-pole, *"One-world Government"*, this multi-national state will be co-operative. Each group, race, and tradition, will govern themselves, based on their personal values and beliefs. The only national, or federally, held beliefs would be those pertaining to: equality, reciprocity, and communities based on the celebration of differences. Reaching this level of harmonious, communal living on a global scale, is shown by the Katari being adorned with the feet of pumas, the wings of the condor eagle, and the antenna of ants. These adornments signify that we have reached the proper maturity and are ready for the great flight.

The beating of these wings will be articulated by harmonious, communal action. This will elevate the Earth and all her inhabitants to a new, luxurious house.

Chapter 3

ANDEAN COSMO-VISION

The Path of the Humming Bird

The Pana, (*phan-ya*) or right-hand side of the path, is considered the masculine side of the path. It governs ritual, initiation, and mystical wisdom. It is the rational, objective, and structured side of the path. This is symbolized by Q'enti, (*k-in-tee*) the humming bird, who unites the material world and the spiritual world. The Pana, is where the paqo learns how to communicate directly with the spirits of the Kausay Pacha. For this reason, it is known as the road to God.

Quite often, this is the starting point for westerners. In the west, we place so much emphasis on intellectual concepts and ideas, that this is where we must start; with what we call the power of the mind, Yachay.

To make the most practical use of this body of knowledge, we must first understand the Andean Cosmo-vision, or the way we see the world. It is a little different than the way modern North Americans see the world. Every culture has its own vision of reality -how we understand the reality is known as a "cosmo-vision." Through this vision, we are taught our ideals and norms.

Quick overview of the cosmo-vision:

All of existence is made up of, and is part of an energy grid, called the Kausay Pacha. The Kausay Pacha is made up of many types of energy. All of these energies are arranged in two categories, according to their quality: Sami, the light refined energies of the universe; and Hoocha, the dense heavy energies of the universe.

There are three worlds, or abodes of energy: The Hanaq Pacha, (the upper-world), which is full of super-refined energies; the Kay Pacha, (the middle-world), a mix of refined and heavy energy; and the Ukhu Pacha, (the under-world), where there is only heavy energy.

We all have a personal energy field that is connected to each other and the earth by lines of energy called, "Seqes." We will now go into more detail about these concepts.

The right-hand path has to do with working from the outside of your bubble, to the skin of your bubble. It is about starting relationships with all the things you feel that are outside of you. This side teaches us how to communicate with the beings of the Kausay Pacha, or, "Living Energy".

The Abundance of Living Energy

This first concept that is sometimes challenging for people is the idea of living energy, or animism. For the indigenous people of the Andes, and to most cultures of the world, all of reality is living energy. You, I, birds, trees, rivers, stars, nature, and the Holy One, are just different forms of living energy.

Kausay is the Quechua word for life, and also, living energy. The Kausay Pacha is the world, or universe, of living energies. The Kausay Pacha, is often seen as a web, or matrix, of life that connects us to each other and the life giving Pachamama (Mother Earth).

The Inka and their predecessors were preoccupied with this energy world, and how our human perceptions of the living energies are related to time/space events in this physical world.

The actual name of this spiritual tradition is the, "Kausay Puriy", meaning to walk or navigate the living energies. Following the Kausay Puriy, one is taught how to stay in a state of harmonious interaction with the energy world. Paqos are first taught how to remain centered in a place of power, tranquility, and beauty -no matter what the situation. This does not mean that a Paqo never feels out of control, powerless, or any darker emotions or impulses. What it does mean, is that we learn to regain our center and harmonize with these feelings and impulses. When we regain our equilibrium, we can navigate the turbulence of our own emotions, thoughts, and situations. Instead of impulsively reacting out of fear, we learn to restore well-being. This can only happen when we learn to accept, harmonize, and love, these darker aspects of ourselves.

Being able to create well-being, no matter what the situation, is a real gift. When we remain centered in well-being, we are in our place of power. From this place, we have something meaningful we can offer the situation. First, we learn to fix the problem in ourselves. Then, we have a greater ability to help others with their problems.

In the west, it is sad to say, there is the predominant view that spirit and matter are completely separated. According to this cosmo-vision, there are three states we live in: the sacred, the mundane, and the profane. I am here to proclaim once-and-for-all, there is only the sacred! In the Andes, there has never been this separation between spirit and matter. We must understand that energy *itself* is conscious and intelligent. These intelligent energies are the creative forces that arrange, organize, and animate all organic matter in the universe. This spirit, or energy, as we sometimes call it, is 100% part of the physical form (person, place or thing) that it comes from. It is also able to transmit itself as a thought-form through space/time, and across any dimensions. This thought-form is known as the Estrella (star form), also known as a Madre. This Madre/Mother does not always look, or act, exactly like your physical form does. Apus (mountain spirits) can come in the Madre forms of: hummingbirds, condors, serpents, jaguars, sometimes other humans, or in an image of a mountain itself. Often times, a person is called to the path after a visitation from the estrella.

The western world has historically discounted this view. Instead of seeing energies as friends to meet and get to know, the West tends to see energies (and most everything) as deaf, dumb, and blind natural resources to be understood, controlled, and capitalized upon.

This view has made it hard for the West to connect with, or even acknowledge, the sacred. This is something that is indeed as simple as breathing. This has also led to a block in our ability to empathize with each other, and to the decay of interpersonal communication. We were taught from early on, not to pay attention to our animal instincts, and consequently, a whole universe of information. This has led to where we now feel great loneliness in this ever-growing world. Trapped in our concepts and expectations of the world, we can be surrounded by a thousand humans, and feel completely alone. As Juan says, "Loneliness is one of the biggest problems facing us today." I believe it all stems from the way the West views reality.

In the modern world, we often believe there is a limited amount of everything. This has led to ideals like the right to life and livelihood. It is relative to how hard you work, or fight, for it. Since there is not enough for everyone, if I get something, then I have something someone else could have had. The Western view takes the concept of limits so far, that it becomes a conceptual prison. Like a stained-glass window, this conceptual prison filters the information we receive from the world, keeping us from being able to see the abundance in our universe. Now, it seems apparent that to feel whole and function freely, we need to re-establish these links with nature, each other, and ourselves.

It is important to note that the West's way of viewing the reality is not wrong. It comes from a very rational place, and has lead to the extraction of the very laws of nature. This has lead to the process of natural science. Now we have all kinds of creature comforts. We have control over the climates of our homes and workplaces. We can preserve foods, allowing us to feed more on less. We have created new forms of transportation, allowing us to travel faster, and in more comfort. We created new forms of communication, allowing us to pass and record information at the speed of light. If we truly look back, we will discover that the average human today has a higher standard of living than the royalty of the 17 and 18 hundreds. All of this comes from our distance from nature.

For all of its good, this view does not lend easily to the ability to see the sacredness in everything. This ability is something that is absolutely necessary for us to feel wholeness and well-being. Stepping beyond this limited view is necessary, if we are to one day have the ability to reorganize our universe beyond the concepts of time, life/death, good/evil, and live in peace with each other.

In the Andean tradition, we believe that though some things are indeed limited, there is an abundance of living energy available. This means an abundance of raw potential, and the possibility of multiple outcomes to any time-space event. We, as humans, have the ability to tap into the raw potential of the universe, taking as much as we like.

For what purpose?

To improve the quality of our life.

Some would argue, if there are these unlimited amounts of living energies, why are we not living fantasy lives? Why are our lives, not as good as we expect? It is because we are behaving according to old ungrounded beliefs. Limiting ideas of what a good life is, what it looks like, or what it should feel like, creates only parameters for that. I have found myself bashing my head against this conceptual wall many times. Times involving day-to-day stresses like, "I need $75 to pay my electric bill or my electric will be shut off." Our minds think, '$75, that's the goal.' We go on formulating all the ways we could make the money. Our minds get focused on the money as the only possible solution to our problem. In a universe with so much abundance, there are going to be many new and interesting solutions. Maybe a friend shows up, and needs a place to stay, and happens to give you the money. Perhaps you need to call to ask the utility for an extension and rely on human kindness. Maybe, your electric gets shut off, and the experience shows you ways to be more self-sufficient. There are a million other ways it could work out.

When we expect a certain outcome, we blind ourselves to other, sometimes better, solutions to our problem. If we are blinded by an outcome that has become unlikely, we can loose our center of well-being, become off-balance, and feel like powerless victims of circumstance.

Industrialized culture has such high ideals, that it often cuts itself off from the natural base. We believe in overcoming nature, instead of being a part of it. We have been taught to hold nature, and our natural impulses, suspect -as something to be outgrown. Even imagination, that spark of divinity within us, is hampered. The result is: that our high ideals have become ungrounded, like a kite with no guide-wire, easily caught in turbulence and often leading to a crash. When one does this they are denying, from the beginning, the acceptance of the amount of living energies and diversity of living energy.

Part of the reason we can not always see this, is that we are trapped in the concepts of positive and negative -mixed with the dogma of good and evil. Thus, in common usage, we have equated good with positive and evil with negative. In the religious ideals that much of the West subscribes to, good is rewarded with life, and evil is punished with death. For the Q'ero, there is no evil, or negative. All of life is light, and therefore, always positive. We acknowledge that all things are not pleasant, but we do not see these as evil. We see this is only "Hoocha", or heavy energy. In the words of Juan, "A box of apples may be heavy or hard to carry, but it is food." This is the same way we learn to look at Hoocha; it is food, or fuel.

An interesting and powerful thing about Hoocha is that it points to our individual uniqueness. You see, what may be Hoocha for you, might not be for me, and vice-versa. Hoocha shows us where we could be more accepting, and in what other ways we can presently grow. Hoocha is an energy-being that only humans create. It is part of our relationship and communion with Mother Earth, Pachamama. Later, in the book, we will focus more on this subject.

Original Virtue

In many spiritual paths, it seems like you are never enough! Your goal: to always purify yourself to be worthy of touching the divine. Elaborate rituals and ceremonials are set up to keep from offending the spirits. Many traditions see the material and spiritual worlds at odds with one and other. There is a belief in the West that spirit finds the material world offensive, unclean, and unholy. This comes from an ingrained cultural belief in "Original Sin".

Original Sin, involves the concept that once the earth was a garden and "perfect". There was no suffering for man in this world. All was "ease, going on smooth." All that the creator asked was that man not eat of a certain fruit, or some other arbitrarily assigned rule. One day, man eats of the fruit, or whatever the "Great Offence" was. When creator asked him about it, he lied and tried to place blame. Humanity's actions so disgusted the creator that he cursed all of creation to become tough on mankind, and all suffering came from this original error. This original flaw and curse, has been inherited by all man and is an everlasting quality of man -along with the curse.

In the Andes, we see the material world as just as holy and spiritual as the non-material. In fact, we see it not as separate from, but as an essential part of the whole spiritual universe. We are on Earth. We live with our mother on Pachamama -the great Goddess's lap. Thusly, we give a lot of respect and worship to Pachamama. It is not a "cursed" place. It is a very important place that all energies visit. It is no mistake we live here; it is quite obvious that we were perfectly made for material manifestation. Earth is a blessing. Pachamama is always looking out for our advantage; she is always trying to make her children's lives easier. It is just about learning to hear and understand her voice. We still live in the garden and in the good graces of the spirits. This is the exact opposite of original sin.

If there is an original sin, then it is the limiting, destructive quality of man's guilty conscious, and the lengths to which humanity will go to deny its own divinity.

In this tradition, we connect with the divine as a way of cleansing our Hoocha, or heavy energy. This allows us to grow in the divine image. We all have an equal right to connect with the energy of the divine. It does not matter how you have lived, are living, or will continue to live your life. It is every human's birth right to commune with, and receive help from, the divine -no matter what your goals.

To us, there is no negative. All of life is light and energy; this can only be positive. We are not naive; we know that unpleasant and uncomfortable things happen. When we see something as negative, we see it as something to protect ourselves from. We try to avoid it; try to get rid of it. When we deny its existence, we disconnect from the free interchange with the Kausay Pacha. In essence, we are throwing up an energetic wall. In this defensive state, our aura functions as a type of jail -imprisoning the heavy energy in our energy body and making it hard to shake or change. Thus, we feel it is being pushed on us or coming down on us. We feel we are a victim to it.

Eventually, if we keep denying something and refusing to harmonize with it, we start to remove our awareness and light from the place it resides in our energy body. This lack of awareness slowly becomes a block that leads to illness. This illness is truly just a communication from our spirit to become aware of, and remove this block, before it threatens our ability to survive.

If we can learn to view this as an energy that is just heavy -or Hoocha, then it becomes just another energy that can be worked with, and re-organized for our benefit. It is useful, even beneficial at times to work with Hoocha. If we qualify these things as Hoocha, or heavy, we can deal with it. The Andean metaphor is: " Carrying a box of apples is heavy, but it's food!" This is how we want to learn to look at Hoocha: as food, as something Pachamama and the Apus can eat. We can also eventually learn to eat, and receive gifts from this.

Seed of the Inka

One of the unique aspects of the tradition is that we believe every person came to Earth with unlimited human potential. This means each of us has the ability to develop the dignity of a king or queen. This idea is called Muju Qoya, or, "Seed of the Inka." Muju means seed, and Qoya is Quechua for queen. This concept is best understood as our seed of personal power. This shows us how we all have the potential -the birthright to become someone like Jesus, Buddha, or Moses in one lifetime. Much of the work of the Paqo, and much of the work in this book, has to do with the accumulation and development of our personal power, germinating our seed, and flowering into glory.

If you truly believe you are from Original Sin, (First Error), then how would you ever be able to trust or believe in yourself? How could you ever believe in your personal power?

Sacred Reciprocity

There is a type of harmony we strive for, a way of life founded by the Inka. In the Q'ero nations, one's very survival depends on this. This way of being, is called Ayni (*eye-nee*). Ayni means, "sacred reciprocity." If you give, you must receive; if you receive, you must give back. Ayni also refers to the quality of our relationships to Pachamama, the nature beings, and the universe itself. This is the one law of the Andean Mystical Tradition.

All humans have four fundamental powers that we use in life. Yachay is the power of mind. Munay is the power of the heart, and Llonk'ay is the power of the body. Ayni is the fourth power, and can be seen as the river whose currents are made of Yachay, Munay, and Llonk'ay. In other words, Ayni is the way in which we express, and the quality of our energetic exchanges with each other, nature beings and the universe. There are many forms of Ayni. Your organs are in Ayni with each other. Human and political relations need Ayni also. It is the principal by which the universe was created, and is maintained.

When Ayni is broken, or we are out of harmony with the natural world, the result can be an accumulation of Hoocha. As the Q'ero say, "Hoocha lands on you."

Please remember, it is one of our jobs as humans to create Hoocha, offering it as food and communication to Pachamama and the Apus. It is also the human's job to find Hoocha that has permeated nature and to offer it to Pachamama. This cleanses and restores the land.

One Western teacher of the tradition, Dr. Alberto Villoldo, states that it is his belief that we are always in perfect Ayni according to our personal growth. Though, I do not totally agree with him on this assertion, I honor this idea, for it frees us from turning Ayni into a type of punishment/reward system.

The Bubble

The Kausay Poq'po, literally means, "bubble," and refers to the field of living energy and information surrounding a living thing. It extends above our heads about a foot. It is about the width of your out-stretched arms, and continues into the earth below your feet, about a foot. The poq'po, is best seen as an organ that regulates the flow or awareness of living energies from the kausay pacha, into your energy body. All things have an energy field, or Poq'po, some traditions call it the Aura, or luminous cocoon. This field of energy is also our field of free will. We have the final say, through our actions and intent, what can and can not enter our poq'po. Even the creator God can not enter our poq'po without our permission. This is why I call it, "The Field of Free Will." Unlike how the aura is often seen as shifting patterns of light, we see the bubble as almost tangible -the outside of it almost like a soap-bubble, or membrane.

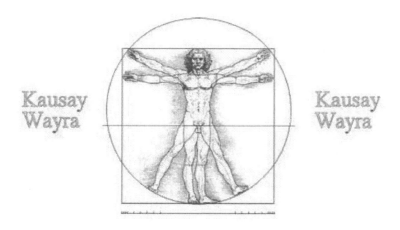

The Bubble is surrounded by the energies of the **Kausay Pacha.** *At the top: Kausay Kanchay, or Light energy; around the sides is Kausay Wayra, or Air energy; below, is the Kausay Pachamama, or Earth energy.*

Attuning Your Bubble

This exercise should be done outside. Finding a place outdoors where you can work undisturbed for a few minutes, stand up and bring your attention to your navel. Try to sense the entire world from the navel. At one point, you will start to become aware of a sphere of sensation around your body. This is your Poq'po, or bubble. Notice your bubble. What impression do you get from it?

- o Is it clear?

- o Is it bright?

- o Is it murky?

- o Is it smooth, or bumpy?

While in this state, with your awareness still centered in the navel, try to sense the sky and note any changes in your sphere. Do this again with the Earth and note any changes.

This is a very good exercise to help you become aware of your Poq'po and the quality of your energy.

The Poq'po can be seen like a soap bubble, with a skin that is sticky like a soap bubble. When two poq'po touch, they become attached by a string or taffy-like pull, created between the two bubbles. This is an example of a Seqe. Through this cord, the bubbles are able to communicate energetically with each other. This is the explanation of how it is possible to sense what someone is feeling, or how you can enter a room where there was just a fight and sense it.

If we see the universe as being made of many strings of living energies, the Poq'po is the place where the strings start weaving together the organism. This is seen as a light, or energy field, around the thing. The Place where all of these fibers enter and start weaving the Poq'po is our navel, called the "Qosqa" (*cous-ca*).

The Qosqa is a very important place to the Kurak Paqo. Not only is it our center of intent, but it is also our main medical instrument. Through training, the Kurak (fourth level priest) learns to travel the universe through these energy fibers. This travel does not happen through spirit-flight or use of psychotropic (as in many other traditions), but through intuitive interchanges with the energy of the fiber. This is much like modern fiber optics, where light and information are passed great distances. You do not need to be in the place the light is made, because through the fiber the light and information is passed and faithfully reproduced in another location. We are all one -woven from the same fibers of the Kausay Pacha -connected through our Poq'po, and can communicate to each other through these energy fibers. These energy fibers are known as, "Seqes."

Types of Energy Lines

A Seqe, is a line of living energy running through the earth, between two ritual sites, spirits, or people. All the pathways that lead to creation are called Seqes. Mountain range uniformity is a Seqe line. Mountains are a geological force of quantum tectonic energy. There are three kinds of Seqe lines:

1.   A Coryana Seqe, is a primary timeless/space less line of creation. It is of a spiritual nature like the Milky Way, a river, or mountain range, similar to lay lines.

2.   A Payan Seqe, is a secondary political line -like those that connect regions of a kingdom. An example of this would be lines of allegiance between a king and his subjects, and even the affiliation between a politician and his party.

3.   A Kaya Seqe, is a social-communal line, like those that connect neighbors, family, and friends. They

are also the lines that connect us to our flocks, fields, and work.

When we connect with the energy field of something, or someplace, through a Seqe, we are connecting directly with the spirit (or Madre) of that thing or place. You don't have to go to the sacred shrine or mountain. We can bring the shrine or mountain to us. When connected with the energy of a place or person, one is also connected with their power.

Paths of the Kausay Puriy

The Kausay Puriy, as practiced by the Q'ero, has two paths: the Pampamisayoq and the Altomisayoq. All of the teachings in this book come from the Altomisayoq path, in particular, the Kuraq (fourth rung) of the Altomisayoq path. The basic understandings of both paths are identical, though the ways of approaching the work is different.

Pampamisayoq literally translates to, "He Who Sits at the Low Table." The Pampamisayoq is the keeper of Earth rituals and ceremony. Accessing the divine through rituals such as: types of divination, Despacho, and pogos,

Altomisayoq literally translates to: "He Whom Sits at the High Table." An Altomisayoq, accesses the divine through their personal energy. All of the teachings in this book come from the Altomisayoq path.

It is important, to note that no priest is higher than the others; all are equal. These branches and levels should be seen less like a hierarchy, and more as personal talents in accessing the spiritual dimensions. Someone who uses ceremony or ritual to heal is no better, or worse, than someone who uses their personal power with the desire to heal. In fact, sometimes a Pampamisayoq can heal a disease that an Altomisayoq cannot. It all depends on whose hands the illness or situation is for. There are times that an Altomisayoq receives their training, and the Karpay from a Pampamisayoq.

Natural Contemplation Exercise

Go outside, center yourself, and look up at the sky. Look for a cloud. With your energy say, "Hello cloud!" Don't think it. Just intend it, and it is done.

Contemplate how your experience of this cloud makes the cloud, and how this cloud's experience of you, makes you.

How you define each other?

How you are both part of a life event? Without cloud, there could not be this life event; without you, there could not be this life event.

We are all necessary threads in the fabric of life that made this event.

Mapping the Universe

In the Kausay Puriy, consciousness expansion is accomplished by mapping the universe. Remember, we are connected to everything and every place by a matrix, or web of life, we call the "Kausay Pacha". We are able to access this web by a process I call, "Natural Contemplations."

Instead of meditation, I see what we do as natural contemplation -something we allow to happen, instead of something we have to force. I see enlightenment as the natural state of a fully developed human. I see the "GOD MIND", Christ consciousness, Krishna consciousness, (Place God-Name here) consciousness", as the natural, primal building blocks of human consciousness that we can tap into when needed.

I tend to see consciousness expansion as the practical, organic growth process of the New Age

Ascension philosophy. Consciousness expansion is the ability to identify "self", or ego, in ever-increasing terms.

Consciousness expansion, frees us from the fear-based paradigm of good and evil. This allows us the freedom to expand in all directions and equate even more with the self and using our thoughts, feelings, and intuition as our guide. This enables us to express our truth, and manifest our personal power.

The great Kuraq, Don Manuel Qespi, was once asked: "*What is the highest spiritual goal of man?*" His reply was: "*To be like a tree, to grow, and grow, and then die*".

All people who start on a spiritual path are searching for, or have had, a mystical experience. The mystical experience is acquired through the displacement of the space-time ego. The ego thusly displaced, allows for a natural consciousness expansion. When we return to space-time, or re-enter our ego, the ego must now grow to integrate this new experience as part of itself.

Our ego can be seen as the instrumental tool through which we manifest ourselves in space-time events. We are not trying to destroy the ego or outgrow the ego. This is impossible if we wish to retain the self. We develop by anchoring our experiences of the divine into our ego. This is consciousness expansion.

Before a person starts on the spiritual path, they are known as a Runa, which means, "human being". Runa, is not a derogatory term, though it is used that way by the upper classes of Peru, when referring to someone of aboriginal heritage. Runa, in Quechua, just means, "Basic Human." When a Runa is called to a spiritual path, they are called a "Paqo Kuna" (nature mystic).

Ayllu Paqo Kuna is the first rung of the Alto Misayoq Path. It is a person who has expanded their consciousness to include the nature spirits of their local environment as part of self. Of these nature spirits, it is of the utmost importance that they connect with the masculine and feminine spirits of their birthplace.

Llaqta Paqo Kuna, is the second rung of the Alto Misayoq path, where a person has expanded their consciousness to include the nature spirits of their city and region.

Suyu Paqo Kuna, is the third rung of the Alto Misayoq path, where a person has expanded their consciousness to include national Apus and Nustas.

Teqsay Paqo Kuna, is the fourth rung of the Alto Misayoq path, where a person has expanded their consciousness to include the Global Apus.

Although there is an elaborate cosmology connected with the Andean path, it is not necessary to convert to follow and grow on the path. The path is quite flexible and inclusive (the Inkan Empire contained over 52 religious groups). All that is necessary is to learn the exercises and practice them. This is why we see it as a spiritual art, much like yoga or meditation, because we can become better at it through practice.

The first thing a Runa learns when entering the path of the Paqo Kuna, are certain basic exercises that allow you to "push the Kausay" (move the "living energies").

Doing the Work: Pushing the Kausay

Learning to work with, and move, the living energies of the universe for communication or practical magic, is referred to as pushing the Kausay. There are many ways to push the Kausay. Pushing the Kausay is a type of art or skill. Like all arts or skills, it is based in your own experiences, and you can get better at it with practice. To truly develop a skill at pushing the Kausay, we must be able to approach it as a child approaches play; this is very important. Among the Q'ero, sacred work is called, "Pukllay." More accurately translated, it means sacred play. It is also the play of children, the play of lovers, and the playing out of rituals. All Andean practices, make up the great cosmic game. All of the techniques are really our toys to play with the cosmos. As Juan says, *"If the sacred work becomes hard work, we are doing it wrong!"* This mirrors the Christian teaching, *"That to enter the kingdom, you must have the heart of a child."*

In the pages that follow, we will go into more detail about the components that make up this art, or skill.

Intent & Perception

According to the tradition, human intent has the ability to drive the living energies of the universe. Now, we need to define intent. What is intent? Too often in our culture, the only use of the word is as an excuse like, "Sorry, that was not my intent!" This is not the only meaning of the word. When I set out to write this book, or to teach a workshop, it starts from intent. In this way, intent can be seen as an arrangement of energy towards a goal. To really drive the point home: move your hand back-and-fourth in front of your face. You are moving your hand with the power of intent. This is what I am referring to, when I say human intent has the ability to drive the living energies of the universe. Remember, the living energies are intelligent. There is no need for mental strain, it is a cosmic game. You just make the intent, and then clear yourself to perceive the fulfillment of the intent. Perception is passive; it is based on experience. Intent and perception are two parts of a whole. We are first active, making the intent. Then, we must become passive in order to perceive the results. Afterward, it is time to make the next intention.

In this cycle, we perform all of our magic.

The 1st Divine Angle: Fathers Rain

The first divine angle, is the movement of energy from God (the upper-world) -a place of perfect refined Sami, through us and into the Goddess Pachamama.

One can receive this type of energy through the top of their bubble and crown of the head. This energy is illuminating, casting the light through our energy bodies and making us aware of Hoocha and/or tension. This awareness, allows us a chance to rid ourselves of the heaviness, and to participate in Ayni (sharing) with our divine Mother Earth, the Pachamama.

Many of the spiritual and religious traditions have this divine angle. It will be very familiar to those who have worked with Reiki, the middle pillar, or many of the other forms of energy healing. In the Western Christian tradition, it is very similar to the idea of working with the Holy Spirit. Don Benito Qorriwaman called it, "Father's Rain" because, like rain in the Mountains, it is soft, relaxing, and cleansing with a downward flow. It is part of our Ayni with Pachamama. Pachamama loves food, and her favorite food is Hoocha; it is like chocolate to her.

When we engage the 1st angle, it creates a type of suspended animation, like floating in water. Just like in a flow of water, the heavier particles, in this case Hoocha, separate and fall towards the Earth.

Saminchukuy

The name of the first angle in the Andean tradition is called the Saminchukuy. Remember, first we make intent, and then we must clear ourselves of doing, and become passive -allowing ourselves to perceive. When you have a perception of your intent, and it does not matter what that perception is, then it is time to make another intention. Please read through this exercise until you are familiar with it:

First, I suggest that you stand. It is much easier to feel the flows of energies when we are standing. Just like in the, "Attuning to Your Bubble" exercise, center your attention in the area of your navel. When you start to become aware of your sphere of personal space, it is time to make the intent to open this sphere above your head. Intend for the flow of Sami (energy from the upper-world) to flow in. Remember, all you have to do is make the intent. The energies we are working with are quite intelligent. They know how to do these things. They only need your permission through intent. Just make the intent, and allow the energy to fulfill that intent. Next, intend that this flow of Sami helps us move our Hoocha towards our feet, much in the same way that heavier sediments are separated and fall in a flow of water. When you have the perception of this happening, intend to close your personal space above your head, and open your field of personal space below your feet. Then, invite Mother-Nature/Mother-Earth, the Pachamama, into your field and offer her your heavy energies as a great gift, and allow her to take it. You do not have to think hard about this, just intend it and let her do the rest. To Pachamama, your Hoocha is like delicious chocolate; Pachamama, she loves to eat, and her favorite food is Hoocha. She is going to take it from you, and eat up all that you are ready to let loose. Pachamama is more than happy to take your Hoocha, but you have to invite her into your space. She won't barge in. She has to be invited, and then you must offer your heavy energy to her as a great gift. You must feel good about giving this to her. Now she will take it. When she has taken all you can simply give, you must refill your personal space by closing our field of energy under our feet, and once again opening above our heads. Allowing the energy from the Hannaq Pacha, to flow in, and fill in the spaces left behind by the Hoocha. Continue to flow these energies until your space is refilled out to the width of your out-stretched arms, and you feel clear and vibrant. This is the basic Saminchukuy.

This is a very simple, but powerful exercise. Practice it until it becomes instinctual. I suggest doing it in multiples of three. This is one basis of all of the energy work of the Andes.

Juan always says, "If this exercise is practiced daily for ten minutes, within two months it can cause an opening in your Qawaq, or seer abilities, to see the energy/spirit-world directly with your physical eyes." Qaway is the power of sacred vision, and a Qawaq is a person who can see the Living Energy Universe with the physical sense of sight. This is only one of the gifts, or toys, of the tradition.

Know that we have given something very precious to Pachamama and she wants to give something back -this is Ayni.

The 2nd Divine Angle:
Mother's Milk

The second divine angle, or movement of the Kausay, is the flow of living energies up from Pachamama towards the sky. Don Benito referred to it as, "mother's milk", because it is empowering. It makes us stronger, healthy, and whole. It can also be seen as a type of blessing. Many spiritual traditions and religions have this angle. Some call it prayer. In the Wiccan tradition, it is called, "raising a cone of power." Within these two angles are the mysteries and abilities of the great "What Is". The creator of a Kundalini yoga school, states that all things are possible while in the flow of the universal energies. All of the Sidhis are available to us during this flow.

For the Andean tradition, these angles are the beginning of an energy-based type of communication. When these angles are placed together, we get a very familiar New Age symbol: the Mer-ka-ba. In more ancient times it was known as the "Clavicle of Solomon".

Siwachukuy

The second divine angle is known as a Siwachukuy. It is Pachamama giving us something back. This energy is enriching and empowering. Before practicing this exercise, I suggest doing the Saminchukuy a few times first. When ready, stand up and center yourself in your navel. Then, when you become aware of your personal space, make the intent to open it below your feet. Then invite Pachamama to reciprocate, and wait for the perception of something gently pushing up on your feet. Make the intention to flow this energy up, around, and through you like a column -allowing it to push up, and out, of your personal space and continue to flow upwards. Flow this until you intuit that it has reached its optimum height. Then, allow the column to recede back down through you, and back into the earth.

The 3rd Divine Angle:
Digestion

This 3rd angle is the horizontal movement of energy. All of the energy used comes from the middle-world. This angle gives us the ability to engage and communicate with the beings of the middle-world, through energy. It is the Art of Compassion, and the act of embrace. Its trans-formative energy, leads to unification, harmony, and growth.

Chapter 4

Connecting to the Sacred Environment

The Inka called themselves, "Children of the Sun." We, and all of creation on Earth, are the children of Inti Tayta and Pachamama. We are their children, and all of the rest of creation are our siblings. We are a big family, with the abilities of our parents to illuminate, harmonize, and empower.

Dialog with Nature

As stated earlier, in our modern world there is such a disconnection to nature, a disconnection to us, and a disconnection from each other.

In the field of Ecology, a dialog with nature is learning the laws of nature and basing our actions accordingly. For our purposes, a dialog with nature is something quite different. It is a metaphor that shows how on certain occasions, mountains can speak to you, and tell you things. Using this approach you can start a conversation with a lake, and that lake can tell you something. Of course, this is not the way of speaking that you and I are accustomed to. It is something tangible, something that can be felt; a communication of spiritual energy.

Nature is our source, the source of our bodies, and the field for the playing out of our experience. The only way to connect with nature, or the spirits of nature, is through the body. The body and the Earth are one. We, in this modern world, have been taught to live from the head, to the point we become stuck in our heads. We have been taught to spend so much time thinking, classifying, clarifying, and evaluating that we have lost the freedom of the experience, and locked ourselves into a conceptual prison. We spend so much time metaphorically trying to break free of the force of gravity, that we have forgotten, it is the loving embrace of our spiritual mother.

The deeper we allow ourselves to settle into and become aware of our bodies, the stronger we connect to nature. The languages of nature are impulse, instinct, intuition, all of which are body based. It also goes to say, the more we tune into nature, the more we understand and clear our own drives and impulses.

As we tune-in progressively more with nature, we learn to honor her cycles and processes; also, we are better able to discover and honor our own cycles and processes. This honoring, leads to having patience with the self, and seeing nature's divinity in the self and others.

Hearing and trusting the voice of nature, we are in a wonderful position where we know that Pachamama, is looking out for our advantage. That she is the source of our dreams, and the power they manifest through. It happens through cooperation. This is not the position of the hard core ecologist; who thinks we do not have the right to change nature, nor is it the position of the radical modernist; who thinks we have the right to change everything. We have the right to change things, with Pachamama's help and direction. You can expect, using this new approach, how nature can tell you how you must behave with them.

Often, we hear how we are killing the Earth. The truth is we can't kill the Earth. We humans just do not have that power. If we did have the ability to harm her, Pachamama is so powerful, that she would shake us off like a bad case of fleas. This is not an excuse to run out there, and pollute without thought of consequence. We do not have the power to harm Mother Earth, but we do have the power to endanger ourselves. We could turn the Earth into a place that is inhospitable to us and biological life like our own, but we can not destroy earth or life itself.

Our disconnection from nature is the cause of much of the physical and social illnesses in our world. A hatred and mistrust of the Earth, is a hatred and mistrust in our selves and our own experience. For we, are part of nature and not separate.

Connecting the Three Worlds

It is common knowledge among the traditional wisdom, spiritual, and shamanic paths that the natural world is made from an overlapping, or weaving, of the three worlds' interpersonal relationships. This actually forms the living time/space universe. Following this understanding, we can see how there are places in the natural world where the overlap is quite noticeable. Our ancestors found these places all over the Earth. They discovered these places had an accumulation of certain energy. Some connected with the upper-world, or beings of the upper-world. Some connected with this middle-world and its beings. Others connected with the lower-world and its beings. These places became the sacred sites and shrines. These are Wakas, (doorways/gates) into the mystical realms. There are two types of Wakas:

Natural Wakas, are places where there is an accumulation of energy.

Man-made Wakas, are places where man has celebrated, honored, or worshiped an energy or entity. They can also be created by repeatedly praying, performing ceremony, or ritual in the same place. You create a doorway to the energies. You are in contact with it, creating a man-made Waka. All churches and temples, are either on the site of a natural Waka, or are a man-made Waka.

When we enter into a Waka, there is an increased chance of an altered state or mystical experience. With the abundance of energy present, there is a natural ease with developing natural contemplation into mystical communion.

Kurak Paqo Don Marcos and I after a late night ceremony.

Phukuy: Ritual Breathing

As the Kurak, Don Marcos and I approached the top of the mist-covered mountain pass leading to the Village of Kiko, all one could see was the faint outline of the cross on the Apuchita -a sacred site marked by a pile of rocks and often a cross. Don Marcos pulled out his llama-skin Coca-leaf bag. I reached in, and picked a Kintu. A Kintu, is a type of mystical offering, using three sacred leafs, (in this case coca) representing our offering of personal power.

I held out the Kintu, and using intent, I thanked the Apus for bringing me here. I asked for their protection and guidance. I raised the Kintu to my lips, breathing my intent into the leaves. The breath carries the intent and energy to the leaves. The leaves then act like a wand, directing the energy to the Apus. I did this three times, offering all of the power of my mind, heart, and body. Then, I wait for the Apu to speak. I feel the Ayni of Apus -soft, subtle, yet powerful. All of the effects of walking the past six hours, at thirteen-thousand feet disappear. I felt strangely energized, while in a state of complete relaxation. I handed my Kintu, now housing the spirits of the Apus, to Don Marcos -who performed his own Phukuy with the Kintu and prays over it. He then brought it to me, and started brushing them across my body, down my chest, arms, and legs. I felt the Hoocha lightening, and lifting off of me -like heat escaping into the cool mountain air. At that moment, it started snowing lightly, then harder. I saw it as a good personal omen, but this site is also one of the first shrines on the pilgrimage to Qori Ritti, the festival of the divine masculine -also known as the snow star festival. I saw this as a blessing from the lord of the Qorri Ritti.

Phukuy, is the ritual blowing of power, or intent, into something. Phukuy is used in various ways. The Ayahuasca-Qero uses it, often with the aid of a tobacco smoke, to invite the spirit of the vine to the brew. It is used as a way of acknowledging thanks for something, such as food or drink. It is used to commune with the tiny spirits that make up a thing. It is used to consecrate an item to use in sacred play (ritual), and countless other ways.

To perform this, you are intending to give your very finest energy with the aid of breath. When we offer in this way, it is an energy encoded communication -explaining why we are initiating the meeting. We do not have to consciously think why we are doing it and just hope the spirits understand. The energy itself is the prayer. Thought, worries, and doubt, only interrupt the flow of this natural form of energetic communication.

Connecting to the Upper-World

Hanaq Pacha (hah-nak pah-cha), the upper-world, is defined by it's abundance of super-refined energy, or Sami. All here is in reciprocity. Some have defined it as the Christian Heaven, though it resembles the idea of heaven, this connection distorts the whole thing. In Christianity, heaven is a reward, a paradise for the worthy and the pure. In the Andean tradition, the upper-world is something quite different. It is every human's birth rite, and every human can connect to it and experience it. The entire way of life is based upon your own perceptions.

To connect and become more acquainted with the energies of the upper-world, we are going to go to a place where there is a surplus of the upper-world energy. Places like churches, temples, or mountains are perfect for this. It does not matter what religion the church or temple belongs to. Many were built on a pre-existing sacred site, or have become a man-made Waka, by the practice of prayer or worship at the site.

After selecting the site, find an iconic feature to work with. It could be the mountain, church, or temple itself. Or, you can choose icons such as statues or paintings of the deity, relics; any spiritual symbolism will do. Perform Phukuy with the object you have chosen. You do not need to make a Kintu (three leaves in a bundle to bless). Just direct your most refined energy of mind, heart, and body towards the object, and send it with a gentle blow.

We are working with energy of the upper-world, where all is in perfect Ayni. So, intend to open yourself and receive the Sami of the upper-world. Then, patiently wait until you have a perception of the flow of living energy from the object back to you.

Stay in this flow, until the flux naturally stops. When the flux stops, the meeting is over. Note that in the flux, there is no need for thoughts, words, visualizations, or visions; you may have them, but they are not needed. Within the flux itself, is the most whole form of communication, spirit to spirit.

Connecting the Middle-world

Kay Pacha, (kai pah-cha) is the world of material consciousness, which is where we live. The "middle" world is filled with both Hoocha and Sami, heavy and refined living energies. Here, reciprocity is exercised through free-will. Sometimes we reciprocate, sometimes we don't. It is the upper part of this world. Where we live has a mix of many types of living energy. This is known as a place of power, and is typically symbolized by the Puma.

Just like connecting with the upper-world, we want to go to a place where the middle-world's energy is prevalent. Lucky for us, we live in this world, so it is everywhere. Pick a place where man's thumbprint is small, and there are a verity of nature beings, (mountains, lakes, caves, fields, hills etc..) and the more nature beings the better. Just like with the upper-world, offer your energy through Phukuy and open yourself. Wait in stillness for the feeling of a touch on your upper forehead between the 3rd eye and the crown. This area is called the Qanchis Nawi, or seventh eye. When you feel that slight touch, intend to flow it through your bubble and body. Continue with this passively, perceiving the flow of energy until the flux of energy ends.

Connecting to the Lower World

Ukhu Pacha, (oohk-hoo pah-cha) is the deep interior world, lower-world, underworld, inside of the planet, and sometimes incorrectly related to the Christian idea of Hell. This is a place of wealth and art. The beings here are much like young children. They have not been taught to reciprocate. Traditionally, this world is symbolized by the serpent.

We are getting close to the time, when the three worlds will become one. This Idea is mirrored in many of the religions.

Just like connecting to the upper and middle-worlds, we are going to select a place where the energies of the Ukhu Pacha, dominate. The best places would be: a cave, mine or deep tunnel. A basement can work as well as any place in nature where there is an opening to the lower-world. This exercise is the same as the last two. Intend to sip in the energies of the lower-world through your bubble.

Rebirth, Waking Personal Power

In these places, like caves, the natural flow of the Kausay Pacha is inward, and into the past. There are a number of ways of connecting to energy. One of these, and a very powerful way, is through memories.

While in the cave, start thinking from the present moment as far back as you can remember. As each memory comes up, note the quality of the energy it brings up in you. If it is Sami, feel it for a moment; then, move onto the next, earlier memory. If it brings Hoocha: note it, give it to Pachamama, and then let yourself move to the next memory.

Keep flowing into the past, memory-by-memory, until you get to the moment of your birth. Afterward, go further to your conception, when the pure-energy of your mother and father, came together with that third energy and became you. Connecting with your mother and father, and giving their Hoocha to Pachamama, ask that they reciprocate by passing down the spiritual gifts of their family lines.

Apu Wamanlipa The sacred mountain of the Q'ero..

Meeting the Apu Kuna

It was late; I had just finished burning a Despacho to deepen and renew my connections with my Ayllu Apus, including Siwa Apu. As I fell to sleep, I instantaneously went into dream.

I could hear a group of people outside my window. It sounded like they were having a party in my back yard. I yelled out the window, "Who's there?" They did not answer back, but I could hear someone storming up the stairs. I did not know who it was, but it was clear enough that they meant business. They came to my front door and tried to open it. Then, a man's voice: "open the door or I will." As the door burst, and he pushed me aside, I came to see a shirtless, overweight man with short, unkempt hair and a crazy look in his eyes. I said, "Who are you?" to which he replied, "You know." I don't know why, I remember being afraid of him, but I went up and embraced him. I then knew without a doubt, that this was my Siwa, sometimes called an Itu Apu. This is the masculine spirit of one's birthplace. For me, this place is Apu Boreman (Fort

Boreman Hill, WV). While in this embrace, he told me he wanted to meet me one-on-one. He asked me what I wished for most in life, and he would go about working it out. Before I could think, I replied, "Help me be a good priest and healer." I was shocked. It was as if I had been waiting for this moment all my life, but unconscious of it. There were a million different answers I could have given. I could have asked to be wealthy, famous, or to have health and a long life. The answer came from some primal energy. I could remember what it felt like to help someone find, or come to peace, with the spirit-world. I knew that when I had spoken it was the true me, and I was proud. Apu Boreman went on to tell me that the noise outside was my Despacho, and they -the Apus, were not done partying yet.

I felt so honored, and I felt another aspect of the power of the Despacho ceremony.

Though the word, 'Apu' actually means, "Masculine Mountain Spirit". The word can also be used as a generic term for all nature beings. Generally speaking, all Apu are masculine, but there are a few feminine mountains as well. Most Apus are mountains.

"Nusta", is the term dedicated to feminine nature spirits, such as: rivers, streams, lakes, and valleys.

Now that we have been working with the energies of the upper and lower worlds, it is time to start connecting with the Kay Pacha -this middle-world where we and the nature beings live. By connecting, I do not mean like in the way of spirit-flight, or journeying. To connect is simply to be in a state of deep contemplation -to become lost in the web of life, the feelings of heavy and light.

To do this, you will need to find a place in nature where there is an abundance of nature beings. A good place is on a hill or mountain. As always, read these instructions until you are comfortable with each step. Place your awareness in your navel, and become aware of your personal space. Intend to open your field, and let the energies of the Kay Pacha to flow in. You will feel a slight touch around the area where your hair line and forehead meet. This is called the Qanchis Nawi, or seventh eye. When you feel this sensation, allow it to flow into your physical and energy body. Allow yourself to get lost in the experience. Don't try to understand or control the experience as it is happening -just be one with it.

Siwa and Pacarina

The first nature beings you will work with are your Ayllu Apu. The most important beings, if you live where you where born, are the Guardians of your birthplace. Your Siwa Apu, sometimes called your, "Itu Apu", is the masculine spirit of your birthplace. So, it is the largest hill or mountain near your birthplace. Pacarina means, "Place of Emergence." It is the Feminine spirit of your birthplace and is the largest body of water, valley or field. If you do not live in the town of your birthplace, plan a trip back to your birthplace someday to taste these energies. These energies are the ones that helped make up your personal energies and there is a lot to find out about yourself from these beings.

Remember that, in this mystical tradition, there are no coincidences. All coincidences point to a greater universal synchronicity. For you to have been born someplace is very purposeful. We do not believe that we choose where we are born, or where we come to live. We are drawn to, and feel at home in, places where our energies and the energies of the nature beings are in some form of harmony. It is the land and nature beings that draw us to them. The nature beings are in charge of the environment -not man.

This is so different then the Western concept of "*Taming the Land*". We may say, "*The Land Tames the Man*". More realistically, we are drawn to the land because our energies are needed to help the land develop as the nature beings want to develop, and it's energy is needed within us for or spiritual growth.

Have you ever noticed how similar people can be who live in the same neighborhoods? I say 'can be', because some people living in a neighborhood are transient. This means they have grown as much as the nature beings in that place can help them grow, and they are awaiting the call of other nature beings that can further their growth. The energy of a neighborhood is the personality of the Ayllu Apus, or local nature spirits, of that area.

We humans are the movers and shakers of the earth and serve as: arms, legs, and the expressive instruments of nature beings. The nature beings are powerful indeed. They have no legs to travel with, but we do. Also, humans have been gifted with a powerful imagination. This imagination makes it possible for us to not only connect with the energy of a nature being, but also to carry that energy with us. In other words, humans serve as a bridge, so that nature beings can connect and talk with each other. We also have the ability to anchor the energies of nature beings to a place (no matter how far in space and time the places are from each other). This creates a seqe, or line of energy, between the places, so they can have a more intimate relationship. We do this with the permission of the nature spirits of both places, and not from our own want to change the world.

Pachamamita and Nusta

Your "Pachamamita", known in Spanish as the, "Sainta Terra" ("Sainted Ground"), is the spirit of your home and the land on which your home rests. She is a very important being in your life. She watches out for you and is instrumental in your life's growth.

I remember being a child, of about ten or eleven, and what was to become my Pachamamita started calling out to me. She called me in dreams and visions. My mother had a job cleaning house for an older, wealthy man. Starting about a year before my father died, I started dreaming about living at this man's place, but it felt like my place in these dreams. I knew, without a doubt, I would one day live there.

About four years after my father's death, my mother and this gentleman discovered a mutual attraction for each other. Though they never married, I considered him my step-father, and he was very good to me. My mother and I moved in with him when I was sixteen. My stay was not for very long. I was young and ready to be on my own.

Years later, I moved back to the land. This time, I lived in an apartment above the garage. This was the greatest time of bonding between him and me. He taught me many things, and much of it had to do with care for the land. He and my mother would work for hours in the yard, on a daily basis. He taught me secrets to growing plants, including talking to them, and a most impressive energy ritual to help them grow tall and fruit largely. He also, once, showed me what I call the, "Lion's Sun Salutation." It was a mixture of deep breathing and slow movements that he did, during sunrise, as a boy. What is amazing is: we are talking about a man born in 1910, in bum-fuck, West Virginia. He had never been exposed to meditation or Yoga. No one had ever heard of energy-work back then, and he was not a religious person. He was very practical and down to earth. He had the heart of a child until his last breath.

A couple years after he died, I found myself moving back into that place again. This time, it was to help take care of my mother. I had been walking the path as a Paqo for a few years at that time. One evening, a year or two later, I had my first real conversation with my Pachamamita. I had many deep conversations with mountains, lakes, caves and fields. However, I had never had a personal one-on-one with my Pachamamita. In rituals and Despachos, I have always invited her in, thanked her with true-love and recognized our mystical connection. This evening, she came to me. It was evening and I was walking through my living room, when I started to notice a presence. It was a soft, comforting, supportive energy. Instantly, I went into a "Qawaq", or a seeing state. I heard a voice say:

"Hello it is time we get to know one and other. I am your mother."

When I say, "hear a voice", I truly mean a felt sense-perception (something very tangible that leads to a synesthesia, or mixture of sensory data). Our intellectual mind then arranges the information into concepts, ideas, language and vision. This is what we call working on the right-side of the mesa. It went on to say:

"I called H.R. to me, because I knew he was driven and would develop me in to what I wanted to be. I also knew he had the energy of success. I knew I could increase his ability to succeed" *When I met your earth mother I loved her honesty, devotion and attention to detail. She learned from H.R how to take care of me. I, in return, through H.R took care of her. It is I who decided she would inherit the land. Now, comes you, my son. I called you for your energy. I know your powers and true dreams, and I want to help you succeed at what you do. You see that is who I am: success and completion. I will teach you how to push through the obstacles in your life. Remember success starts at home. I have always been a part of H.R., your mother, and you -and you are a part of me."*

This experience took me back to my youth. I remember how I used to know, and talk, to the

Pachamamita of my grandmother's land. Marble-white and lime-green is how I knew her. I could remember the Pachamamita of my childhood home; I knew her as wild, free darkness. I could remember the calming peace of the Pachamamita the graveyard up the street, and the spirit of the park near my house. I also remember how the Pachamamita would transform herself into imaginary friends that I played with. You see, this path is not really about teaching you new things -it is more about reminding you of what you already know.

Being a Good Host

A large aspect of doing the work, is that we never work alone. We exist in both a seen, ordinary universe, and an unseen, non-ordinary universe. As we set out to perform a ceremony, or spiritual play session, although we may be unaware of it, there are a number of beings watching us (that could be working with us). There is the Pachamamita, or the feminine spirit of the land, you are working on. There are: Apus and Nustas of the local ecosphere, Wyra (the spirit of the wind), Inti Tayta (Father Sun), Pachamama (Mother Earth), Mama Killa (Mother Moon), Phuyu (the clouds), Ch'aska or Estrellas (the stars), Chaw (the day), Tuta (the night), Wiraqocha (the creator), and our ancestors. These are all present as soon as we start our spiritual play session. They see it, and in it, a chance to be in communion with us. They know this type of play very well and are always there to help us, but because of the field of free will, the effective influence and guidance of these beings is minimal. This is so, until you invite them into the work, and start your relationship or communion with them. We need to ask for their help.

Being a good host is something we learn to do, it is an art and with practice, we get better. A good host seeks to know/learn more about those being hosted. A good host acknowledges your existence, your likes and dislikes, and tries to provide the things you like to make you comfortable.

The simple act of acknowledgment is big part of hosting. Words are powerful magic. We created names, and consequently words, as a way of expressing power.

Think about it.

Words started as a need to express power to one another. Words are an example of thoughts made manifest, but they are much more then that. Words can be seen as a man-made seqe. Words are strings; that's how they work. They connect things together. The power, or Quanta, that enlivens them comes from the thing the word symbolizes. This is colored by the intent, and emotional tone, of the person uttering them. The word brings a bit of the power it expresses.

For example, I say the word, "love." In this case, you read the word, "love." The word brings a bit of the energy of the spirit of love with it. You and your nervous system are changed by the word. Maybe visions, memories, and concepts come to mind. This all was initiated by the word, or I should say the power encased in the word.

All words are persons, when you speak them you are surrounding yourself with the influence of these persons. You surround yourself constantly with word-spirits. The emotional intent with which you utter words, creates the emotional quality you are surrounding yourself with -their emotional quality/the type of influence they have on your living reality.

Choose your words wisely, especially when involved in spiritual-play sessions.

Confidence

Confidence is a wonderful attribute to have in most aspects of life. In this path we say, "Work with confidence, or don't work at all."

What is confidence?

It is being authentic. It is developed from knowing who you are, and accepting yourself as something beautiful. Confidence comes, partly, from knowing you are part of the family (whose head is creator) and siblings with all of creation. Confidence is being yourself, and knowing the spirit-world will accept you just the way you are.

You will know when you have developed confidence, because you will feel the comfort you feel with your best friends and family, when communing with the spirit-world. Confidence will grow as you do self-exploration and ritual work. We don't always feel confident enough -those moments take courage to push through our doubts.

Courage

It takes a great deal of courage and strength to walk the path of living energies and speak your truth. All of the intuition and guidance in the universe is impotent, if you do not have the courage to act on it. We are always pushing our limits and that takes courage. Not everyone in the world has had a mystical experience. If someone has not had this type of experience, they cannot relate or understand this type of thing.

One of the first limiting fears you must find the courage to overcome is: the fear of being crazy. Let me put this one to rest:

You are crazy!

I'm crazy!

However, there is important work to be done in the crazy!

The next limiting fear, is the fear of being wrong. This fear will impede your walk on the path. We are learning a primal way of approaching reality. Many of us have not approached the world in this way since we were children. Back then, our knowledge, wisdom, and understandings were very limited. Our imaginable minds were wide-open and intuition was a way of life.

Respect

Respect comes from truly knowing yourself. When you know your true identity, as an integral part of the living universe, you also realize everything's true identity as a non-diminishable part, a thread in the fabric of life.

Respect is the acknowledgment that the longer we live -the more we have grown and learned. Someone that has lived even a day more than you, and has seen more life, deserves respect. This does not mean that they are necessarily wiser. It does mean, that we owe them the benefit of our doubt.

Respect is not earned. It is an inalienable rite of all life. Respect cannot be lost, or gained. When people say they have lost, or gained, respect in you -what they truly mean is that their opinion of you has changed. Opinion and respect are not the same thing.

Love

Love is a power. This is better stated as: the ability to give and receive love, is a power we call, "Munay". All aspects of a Paqos life spiral around love. The love I speak of is not the romantic idea of love. Every Paqo manifests love in a different way. Love can be cold, or warm, for instance.

Self-love must come first. Love comes from knowing yourself, and seeing yourself (the good, the bad, the beautiful, and the ugly) as a living miracle. When you fall in love with yourself you know love as a choice -something you can turn on and off.

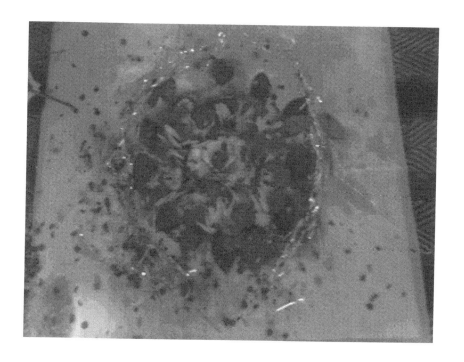

Chapter 5

The Pachamama Despacho

Rituals and ceremonies play important roles in the wisdom traditions. Not only do they commemorate the occasion, but they also play the role of honoring the spirits that naturally influence and make up the occurrence. For this reason, rituals hold within them the secrets of the primal sciences. This is a beautiful way of recording information and teaching wisdom and knowledge. Through rites, knowledge is passed, natural forces acknowledged, communion is established, and wisdom is found.

There is a natural process, hidden in the ritual progressions of our ancestors, that is used to initiate us to the deeper aspects of life.

The Despacho is the most common ritual in the Andes. It can be either a gratitude bundle, or a request for a blessing. Despachos are buried in the earth or burnt when they are completed as an offering to Pachamama.

You will need:

- A rectangular piece of white paper.

- A shell (clam shells are ideal) -representing the feminine, the cosmic circle, wholeness.

- Sugar.

- 22 fresh plant leaves, especially Coca, laurel, olive, sage, or bay, in as perfect as possible condition.

- Red flowers -any number. Red or rainbow thread to tie the Despacho closed.

- Cookies, peanuts, raisins, dates, coca seeds, wafers, chocolate, candies, etc...

- Symbols of Mother Mary.

Optional items:

- White cotton to represent clouds.

- Colored threads or yarn -to represent the rainbow.

- Tiny squares of silver and gold foil/paper. Silver represents feminine energy and the Lloque -left-side of the sacred path; gold represents masculine energy and the Pana -right-side of the sacred path. It is usual to place both colors in the Despacho.

- Paper figures representing people, animals, keys, houses, and so on.

- Sacred plant items, such as seeds, grains, grasses, herbs, and so on may be used. Sage, sweet-grass, and tobacco are common. Food items are important to feed the spirits, especially bright colored candies or sweets. Small stones or stone fragments are great -Meteorites are very powerful offerings! Fragments of natural items, such as animal fur, teeth, or claws are also nice.

1. Take a moment to prepare yourself for entering sacred space: orient your mesa to the six directions, connect your Seqes, open and spread your mesa.

2. As you offer an item to your Despacho, you infuse it with your finest intent, by allowing the Sami of the thanks or blessing to first fill you, and then infusing it into the items by gently blowing on it three times before you place it in the Despacho. Place the shell on the white paper, with the "bowl" of the shell facing up. Place the cross in the bowl of the shell.

3. Make 11 k'intus, (or leaf-prayers) -the usual number made in offering to Pachamama. Each k'intu is made up of two leaves, stacked neatly one on top of the other. In a Despacho for Apu or for both Apu and Pachamama, you offer three leaves for each Kintu. As you make each leaf-stack, hold it up and pray over it, breathing prayers through them with a soft breath. Place

each completed k'intu, moving in a clockwise direction, like rays around the central shell.

4. Next, offer the flowers, or the petals of the flowers -arranged in a pattern on top of the Despacho that seems good to you.

5. Offer the optional ingredients, according to your personal intention and preferences. Be open and loving with each item as you offer it to the Despacho. Take your time and use your intuition. When it is complete, close the Despacho by folding the side corners in first, then the bottom corner, and then the top corner down to, "close the mouth." Tie the Despacho with red thread.

6. Take your Despacho to the place where you will be burying it, consciously make the offering, with reverence, as you place it in the earth.

The Ceremony of Kintukuy

Every year on the first of August, we spend the day remembering the deity Pachamama. It is a time for reuniting to family. At this time we also make a special type of Pachamama Despacho, placing offerings of flowers, leaves of coca, seeds of maize, chicha of jora, etc. This is a time for being thankful for food, health, fertility and life. Many, incorrectly, call it a, "payment to the Earth." This is false, because our mother would never place a price on her love. The ceremony of offerings to Pachamama is called, "Kintukuy". It is a gratefulness act, and receives its name because it consists of making clusters of coca leaves, called "kintu". It loses its value if it is reduced to a superstitious act. That is to say, if you do it from fear, to hold-off the misfortunes that could come like punishment, it is not being done in the right spirit.

How to do Kintukuy?

The ceremony of Kintukuy is perhaps the most beautiful ceremony created by the Andean ancestors and has been transmitted from parents to children through many generations. Within the year, it falls on two important dates: the first of August, and the second of February. In August, it is dedicated to our earth Mother (Pachamama) and in February, to our water mother, (Yaku Mama or Qocha Mama).

The details in making this ceremony are simple. What is most important, is that the family is reunited and is thankful to Pachamama, with small offerings thrown with devotion to the fire, or buried in a discreet place. One shares, with joy, plates of food and a little maize drink, Festejando. This is on the day of our Mamacha (madrecita).

There are seven main stages that must be fulfilled in a ceremony of Kintukuy. This follows the tradition conserved by the great Yachayniyuq teachers of the provinces of Paucartambo, and Canchis of the Cusco region.

1) Selection and cleaning of the home.

2) Conduction of the ceremony and location of the participants.

3) First oration: connecting Seqes to the greater deities that are asked to come.

4) Second oration: Handing out the K'intus to each participant.

5) Third oration: Closing the offering (Despacho) and spiritual cleaning of the participants with the Despacho.

6) Giving the Despacho offering to Nina (the fire).

7) Final hug, the sharing of positive energy with each other, and extending those positive feelings into the future.

According to our tradition, the ceremony of the Kintukuy is to be made on the first day of August, although it can take place on another day of the same month. In the Andean valleys, in the south of Peru, it is the seed-time of maize. In order to feed us, Pachamama enters a period of fertility and welcomes the seeds placed in the small farms. The night is used for this ceremony, due to the necessity of silence for the oration and concentration of the mental energy. When this ceremony is organized by the director of a community, with the purpose of protecting the edges of their communal territory, it is accompanied with music and dances that expel sadness and other feelings.

Chapter 6

Art of Personal Power

In this section, we will open the knowledge of accumulating and developing personal power. First, we must understand what personal power is, the ways in which we lose it, and what are the steps to regaining our own personal power.

Simply put, personal power is our feeling of well-being. There are three components to well-being: mental clarity, emotional tranquility and physical comfort. Each of these components are power, in and of themselves, to be developed and used. Every human being has varying mental, emotional, and physical capacities. All three aspects are always active and working together. These three are fundamental and universal. We each have one of these powers that are predominate in our lives, and is used as the main means of exchange with our personal reality. This center is where the information we are receiving from our energy universe is being organized into our perceptions. Each of us organizes our world either through our mind (thoughts), our heart (feelings), or through our body (physical productivity) -a mix of two or even all of these. None are better then the others. All are equal. This is just one more of the many ways our spirit expresses our uniqueness and individuality.

In North America and Europe, we put a great amount of emphasis on the mind. That is not to say on intelligence, logic or reason, but on supremacy of cold calculation, over feelings or actions. In Peru, the emphasis is on feeling; in Asia, it is on productivity. This is of course a generalization, and is not to say that there are not physically guided people in North America, or heart guided people in Asia. There is a mix everywhere. My point is to show the qualities that are culturally emphasized.

We all have access to these three centers, but each of us is primarily comfortable with one. Knowing your primary center of perception helps you to develop balance, and also see the barrier that's blocking the way to full body awareness. We start by developing our predominate power. The end goal is to develop all three as far as possible. It is necessary that they all three are working together, to create a harmony between thought, feelings, and action -also known as the game of relations.

We will now go into more detail on each of these three powers, stances, or centers of exchange, as they are sometimes called.

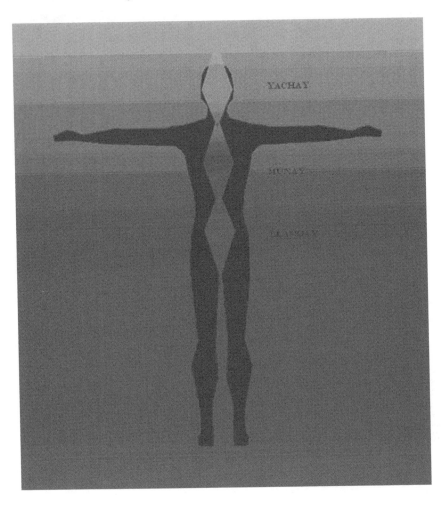

To show these on the body imagine: 3 big diamonds vertically stacked one on top of the other. The top diamond is roughly the head, the middle is heart-center, and the lowest is the core.

Yachay

The power of the mind is the ability to learn, know, remember, and the capacity of being flexible in thoughts and action -not being controlled by opinions and judgmental behavior. The growth of Yachay, is from raw knowledge, to being able to shift through the facts and arrange that knowledge into practical formulations that enrich all aspects of life. This is known as growing the roots of knowledge into wisdom or truth. Creator gives everyone a unique journey through life, so the truth is relative to our experiences. What is the truth for me, may not be the truth for you -and that is o.k. We need to develop the confidence and strength to trust ourselves. Also, we need to live and express our personal truths. Yachay, is also the amount of wisdom gained through our personal journey.

Munay

Munay is the power of love and will together; it is not romantic love, but more of a compassionate, loving kindness. Munay can be seen as the all-encompassing power of unconditional love and our capacity to love. It develops from a sober will -meaning our actions are not based on impulsive, emotional behavior. To cultivate this, we must move beyond our personal past. As Munay grows, so does our ability to do deliberate acts of loving kindness. Taking care of plants, animals, and other humans, helps the accumulation of Munay. Munay is also the ability to love and be loved, gained through our personal journey.

Llankay

Llankay is the power of physical work. All work, including mental, creative, ceremonial, and sacred work. It is your particular way of crafting reality. It is also the refinement of touch. It is your power to do, and influence, things physically in the material creation. Llankay, is also the power of drive -to push yourself physically to accomplish your goals.

A Brain Map of Creation

All parts of creation hold allegories for a nature mystic. In this part, we will be looking at the allegories hidden in the structure of various brain types. Many anthropologists believe the Inka could perform brain surgery.

Like the brain, all things in nature contain allegories to the divine reality of existence.

The Serpent Brain

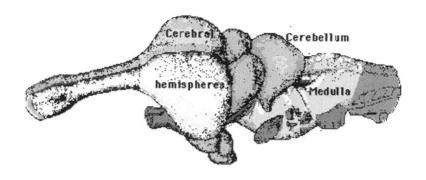

The serpent brain is small, most of the time the size of a walnut, but it is all you need to thrive in this world. The serpent brain connects us to fluidity, fertility, obscurity, the forces of nature, and cycles of water. It is associated with sound vibration, instinct intuition, and impulse. It connects us to the ancestral memory and collective unconscious. It is associated with Llankay and the power of physical motion. The serpent brain is naturally connected to the Ukhu Pacha, or underworld.

The Mammal Brain

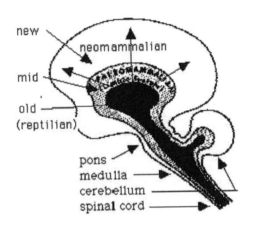

The mammal brain extends from the reptile brain and has a more fully developed mid-brain. This gives mammals the ability of mastering the different senses, deeper emotions and larger emotional connections. Leading to the ability to recognize similarities, create trust bonds, and group together in herds. It is associated with Munay the ability not only to perceive feelings and emotions, but to also express these feelings as action. The mammal brain naturally connects to the middle-world or Kaypacha. It lends itself to "Us" and "Them" mentality, herd mentality, the four fs fighting, fleeing, feeding and reproduction.

The Bird Brain

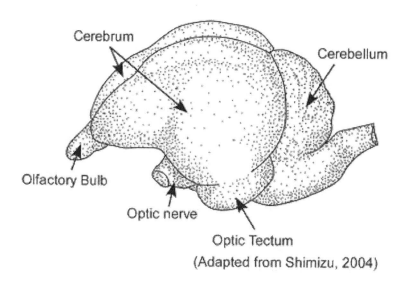

(Adapted from Shimizu, 2004)

The bird brain is involved with clarity, structure, and fecundity. It is associated with sight, spatial awareness, and complex navigation. This brain is associated with Yachay: the power of mind/higher thought. It is also involved with the ability to functionally use mathematic abstractions and models. The bird brain is naturally connected to the upper-world, or Hanaqpacha.

Human Brain

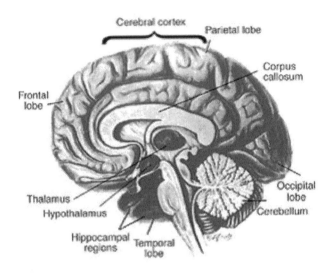

The human brain is a unique type of mammal brain that combines all qualities of the reptile, mammal, and bird brain. It also includes the most recent adaptation, known as the Neo-cortex, located in the frontal-lobe of the human brain. This brain configuration gives humans the ability for complex problem solving, deeper empathic abilities, and higher cognition. It lends to the capacity to live harmoniously in large groups, working together to accomplish common goals, the ability to contemplate abstractions and understand the laws of nature. This powerful instrument is what fostered the development of the natural sciences. Associated with

Ayni, and Taqe (reciprocity and harmonious interactions), it also is associated with Tawantin -or the, "Four United Together." The very configuration of the human brain, the store-house of consciousness, hints at the Teripaypacha -a time when the the upper and lower-worlds will spill into the middle-world.

Languages of Self

Here, we are talking about the languages of creation, and the self. Alberto Villoldo likes to describe them like Russian nesting dolls, each contained within the next. Each language works like a blueprint, or matrix, to inform the languages before it. The languages of self are a model to help us to understand various ways healing and illumination can take place.

Biochemical - This is the language of the body, and has to do with the literal level of matter. This language is physical, chemical, and cellular. This is the language that is used with modern medicine.

Phonetic —this is the language of words, concepts, feelings and ideas. This is the symbolic language of the mind. In healing, this is the language of Psychology.

Images — This is the mythic language of the soul. It involves archetypal icons that convey more then what is seen. For instance, the way looking at fine art can inspire the soul. Also, it is the way spiritual teachings can illuminate us to life's deeper mysteries

Energy — the essential language of spirit/the 4th level language. The all-inclusive language that makes you feel at "one" with the universe. Very deep spiritual teachings are disseminated energetically.

Energy is the master matrix or blueprint for all the other languages. If you where to make a change on the energy level it trickles down, re-informing all the other language levels.

Developing Personal Power

Just like the seasons, our lives move in cycles. As the cycle returns, it is necessary to reconnect, acknowledge, and gratefully honor the wisdom/spirits that have supported and guided us. Through the simple act of acknowledgment and thanks, our intentions weave a stronger filament with the wisdom threads and spirits. In essence, this acknowledgment and honoring is also the renewing of our relationships with the wisdom and spirits for another cycle. This action is symbolized in the Despacho ceremony. In this circular way, life is polishing and turning us into, "Yachayniyuq" ("person that has knowledge"). Deep knowledge (Yachay) only prospers on the roots of our heart (Sonqo). This deeper heartfelt knowledge is tested in the laboratory of life, growing inwards and outwards, like the roots of an old tree. This practice leads us to become a, "Munayniyuq" ("person that takes in their heart the force of munay").

Munay is the capacity to give love and affection. Through the development of Munay, one arrives at a state of universal love that can see beauty in all things.

When the Yachay has been enriched with the development of the heart, the two work together creating a type of superior loving consciousness. This practice of love-consciousness leads us to becoming a, "Llankayniyuq" (a person with the power to act). This developed form of Llankay is always preformed in the spirit of loving kindness, with great concern for the growth and well-being of others, including nature. As you can see, the powers build on each other to reach their full development. Once developed, these powers become qualities in us that empower our personal interactions with each other, the nature beings, and the spiritual world. In this way, they enrich, and help to facilitate, our ability to stay in Ayni with the universe.

We can understand this further in the metaphor of a river. Ayni can be seen as the movement of the river, from one place to another. The internal currents of this river are Yachay, Munay and Llankay. As the river encounters obstacles, if the currents are not powerful enough, then movement becomes blocked; the water stagnates. It is the power and flow of these currents that navigates the obstacle, so that the movement of the river continues freely.

Continuing with this metaphor, as the current navigates the obstacle, the churning created (internal movement) helps to cleanse the water. By slowly dissolving the obstacle, it enriches the river with minerals that are then passed with the current to enrich others.

We are like that river. Our ability to share our authentic self with others is dependant on how well we are able to navigate and harmonize the obstacles in our life (mental, emotional, and physical).

This is where the idea of Ayni, becomes something greater than the ability to share, and we begin to glimpse it as a universal law.

Limiting Potentiality

We all come to this world perfect -full of personal power. Though undeveloped, we have unlimited potential for development. Of course, we are not truly equal. We are each born with unique abilities, talents, and handicaps. This is decided by the universe and our personal heredity to help us develop our own individuality. This strengthens our need for one another, and our capacity to accept differences, creating healthy communities. We are all born with equal potential to develop into a powerfully unique person.

As I stated earlier, in the Q'ero Nations, the mere fact you exist gives you a right to life. Your flaws are part of your uniqueness. I remember, in the village of Kiko, I met a mentally handicapped girl. She was mute, and could only express herself through primal emotional outbursts and sounds. Unlike in the Western cultures, where she and her experience would be seen as invalid, she was a respected and necessary member of her community. The Q'ero did not look at her with shame, fear, or pity. They did not try to quiet her emotionally charged expressions, but accepted them as part of her whole uniqueness. Her energy made everyone close to her smile and glow -including me. It was not out of a place of superiority, but from a place of love and gratitude that she existed. She, like the Apus that surround her village, had the natural ability to lighten moods, and bring a sense that all was indeed in order with the world.

In most of the modern world, and surely many places in the past, there are limitations that we are taught to put on ourselves. These limits block our development. Where do these limitations come from?

They come from our self-conscious and self-critical mindset. Instead of viewing our mistakes and failures as parts of our whole, unique self and harmonizing with them, we see them as things that are negative and subtract from our wholeness -and even our right to life. This can create an inability to trust and believe in ourselves and our experience of the world.

We are taught almost from birth, to view our authentic self as a powerless victim of circumstance. We are taught to see power as an outside influence, not as something innate. This state leads to a view of power as something limited that you fight for and hold over others —to help carve your way through the big, bad world. Seeing power as something that gives you a greater right to life then others, instead of something you have to share with the world for the enrichment of all, is an askew view of power. This leads us to see the world as a competition, a battleground for power, and other humans as suspected usurpers of our power and well-being.

One of the first powers we discover is the ability to make another person feel less than human/subservient to us. In this way, we are always undermining each other through the tactics of alienation/negation of other's experiences. We undermine each other, especially those that appear different from the "Us" status-quo. Society tends to undermine those that have a view of reality that challenges our culturally held view, especially those that are proud in themselves for this difference. We are taught that differing views are dangerous to the community, and that self-pride is the root of all undoing. This is classic herd mentality, or the "Us" and "Them" game. This type of behavior has, at its root, fear.

I am happy to say, humanity is at a place in its evolution where we are overcoming our fear-based behaviors. This is also the work of the 4th level, or the Kurak: to overcome fear. This does not mean that fear will be destroyed. Fear is a necessary part of our whole -as is anger. It means we are clearing ourselves, so that we do not behave out of these places in day-to-day life and create cycles of abuse.

The Chaupi

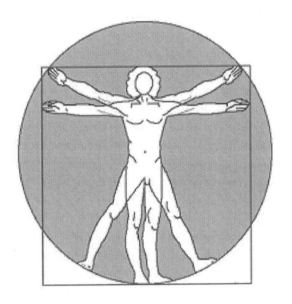

The Chaupi is the work from the skin of your bubble to the skin of your body. It has to do with the awakening, and use, of a set of perceptive energy-eyes. Also, it pertains to working with group energies. This side has to do with socio-relationships not based on roles, but on flows of energy. We are learning to perceive this living, breathing world as flows of the Kausay Pacha.

Chapter 7

The Right and Left-sides of the Work

There are two sides to the sacred path of the Inka and Q'eros. These are sometimes called working the "right" and "left" sides of the mesa. The right-hand work is considered the ordinary work. It involves communication with the spirit-world and relationships with spirit/nature beings. The right-side is the path of the mystic. The teachings of the right-hand side lead to the ability to actually meet and communicate with the Madre or spiritual beings of the Kausay Pacha. Male Paqos are said to have a natural talent with working the arts of the right-hand.

The left-side of the sacred path has to do with working outside of the ordinary. It involves how to use the power of the spirits for practical pursuits, such as healing, or divination. The teachings of the left-side have to do with the ability to handle the power of the Kausay, and to use it for this practical magic. Women are said to have a natural talent for working the left-side.

In the end, it is the Paqo's job to learn to work both sides of the mesa. Working only the right-side of the tradition, leads to dry, dead ritual. While working only the left-side, becomes chaotic creation. When we develop both sides, we can enliven our rituals with vital energy. We can also learn to organize and direct the chaotic, creative potential.

Bridge between the Right and Left

The right-side of path always deals with ritual knowledge, philosophy, and initiation. The right-side teaches you how to commune with nature spirits to ask for help and guidance.

The left-side always deals with magic, healing, developing your intuitive ability, and power.

There exists a bridge between the two: it is called, "Chaupi", and every Paqo owes it to their self to develop both as much as they can. The power of the Chaupi is called, "Munay." "Munay" is the power of love and will together. It is fully developed by falling in love with yourself and the expressing that self-love to others.

In our tradition, Munay, is the bridge between the hemispheres of the brain and action (the right and left sides of the path).

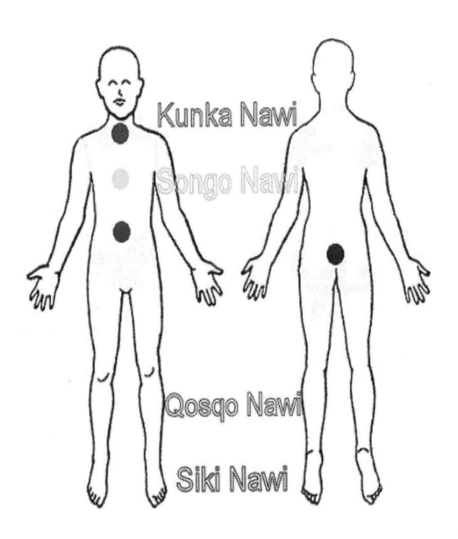

Nawis

The word, "Nawis", is Quechua for "eyes" -both physical and spiritual (energetic) eyes. The human body has 7 energy nawis, similar to the chakra system but not entirely the same. For us, these eyes are not just energy doorways, but specialized perception organs that allow us to perceive and communicate with different realms of energy.

Siki Nawi- The eye at the base of the spine. Its color is black, and it connects us with the energies of water.

Qosqo Nawi- Centered near the navel, this eye's color is red. It connects with the realm of Pachamama (Mother Earth).

Sonqo Nawi- Located in the chest, its color is gold. It connects us to the realm of Inti Tita (Father Sun).

Kunka Nawi- Located in the throat. Its colors are blue and silver. It connects us to the realm of the Wyra (Sister Wind) and Mama Killa (Mother Moon).

Pana Nawi- This is our right eye. Its color is gold. It connects us to the realm of Inti Tayta, and our mystical vision.

Lloque Nawi- This is our left eye. Its color is silver. It connects us to the reality of Mama Killa and our magical vision.

Qanchis Nawi- This is our seventh eye. It starts at the third eye, and reaches up to the top of our heads. Its color is purple, and it connects us to the realm of upper-world.

Opening of the Qosqo

Up to this time, we have been using the bubble itself to connect with the Kausay Pacha, Apus, and Nustas. We do this by opening the bubble when we are in a place where these energies are naturally prevalent. We accomplish this by doing a Despacho, calling the energies to surround us, or going to a Waka. We can also do this by going to the nature being's bubble, connecting directly, and allowing the energy to flow through. The energy flow is a communication.

Just as there are sacred sites, "Wakas", on the earth, we -being the children of the earth, also have sacred sites on us. When we are talking about the sacred sites of the human body, we call them Nawi (eye).

The first Nawi we work with is the Qosqo Nawi. Qosqo means, "navel", or umbilical cord. This is also the meaning of the name of the town of Cusco, Peru -the capital of the Inka Empire.

The navel was our first eye, the first connection to the reality, and our first instrument of intent and perception. When we needed something, we expressed it through the Qosqo. When we were given something, we received it through the Qosqa.

At birth, the physical Qosqo to our human mother was cut. However, the spiritual/energy Qosqo, connected to our spiritual mother, was never severed. One may be a little out of practice with using it, but this technique can easily be developed.

To find the Qosqo: shut your eyes, take a few deep breaths, and center your awareness in your stomach. You will start to notice the sphere of sensation and personal space around you. Start to slowly move your hand up and down, palm toward you, in the region of your navel. Keep your hand about two-to-three inches from the body. We are looking for a place that causes increased sensation in the hand. This place is the Qosqo.

To open the eye of the Qosqo, find the Qosqo with your hand. Slowly increase the distance between the Qosqo and the hand in about two-inch intervals. At each interval, stop, and make sure there is still a connection of sensation between the hand and Qosqo. If the sensation becomes weak, make the intent to reach up to your hand, from your Qosqo, and wait for the sensation to increase. When you reach a distance of about a foot, the Qosqo Nawi (eye) will naturally open.

To develop the ability to open and shut the Qosqo at-will: Start moving the hand back towards the body -closing the Nawi. Note the sensations in the Qosqo. Notice how it feels in the navel, for the Nawi to be closed. Then, slowly move the hand back away from your body. Note when the sensations in the Qosqo change. This is when the Nawi opens. Hold the hand at this distance; make a mental note of the distance your nawi opens. The distance differs from person to person. Move the hand back-and-forth from your body -noticing sensations of the Nawi opening and shutting. When you are able to tell the difference between the Qosqo Nawi being open and shut, it is time to work on opening the Qosqo nawi without the aid of the hand.

Learning from Pachamama

There are many things we can learn from Pachamama. As our mother, she is one of the best role models, reflecting to us our powers and potentials.

We are naturally connected to Pachamama, and the whole Kay pacha, through our Qosqo. Our Qosqo is a direct line to our mother. We just need to strengthen that connection and relearn that energetic language.

Lying, navel down, on the earth is healing and invigorating. As our navel touches the earth and we relax, there is a natural release of accumulated Hoocha. As this is occurring, Pachamama goes about the business of cleansing and harmonizing the Seqe (energy lines coming into our body). This natural phenomenon is the basis of communication with the nature beings.

Chumpis

In Quechua, the word Chumpi means, "belt". Each Nawi has a belt that develops around it in the same color as the eye. The knowledge of the Nawis and Chumpis is part of a very rare sect of priests called the Chumpi Paqos. They are so rare you can hardly find one in Peru. Many Western teachers have been trained as Chumpi Paqos, including myself. I have not found many Q'ero who have much knowledge in this branch. My initiator, Juan, had received the initiation from both of his principal teachers, the famous Paqos: Don Benito Qoriwaman, and Don Andreas Espinosa.

The tool of the Chumpi Paqo (Priest of the Belts), are a special set of five stones called Chumpi Khuyas. Just as there are five different stones, there five energy belts. The five energy belts correspond to the seven energy centers of the human body. They roughly relate to the seven major chakras.

Each belt contains an eye, which is a center of perception that is opened by the Paqo's chumpi khuya. The advancement or development of the eye of perception is left up to the discretion and responsibility of the individual. The opening of the eyes is called the Nawi Kitchay.

The ceremonial weaving of the belts is called, "The Chumpi Away", or, "Belting Ceremony." The Chumpi Away initiation causes healing and balancing in the self. This initiation is powerful in removing the heavy energy (that we have accumulated living in a cultural environment that supports the development of our soul separate from nature). This ceremonial ritual is an example of how an individual can be reconnected to the living energy of Kausay -restoring your natural rhythms and cycles, with the rhythm and cycles of nature.

The first energy belt activated in the Chumpi Away is called, "Yana Wara". The color associated with it, is black. Its center is the Siki Nawi -at the base of spine. The black belt is associated with water and the flow of our impulses.

The next is Puka Chumpi. The color correlation is red, representing the blood of Mother Earth, Pachamama. Its center is the Qosqo Nawi, located at our navel. It corresponds with the element of earth, and our emotions.

The third belt is called, "Qori Chumpi". It is the gold belt. Its center is the Sonqo Nawi, located in the chest. This belt is associated with the Sun, Inti Tayta. The perceptual quality corresponds to the feeling of love.

The fourth belt is the "Qolque Chumpi." It is the blue or silver belt. Its center is the Kunka Nawi, located in the neck. This centre is associated with the element of the Moon (Killa), and the air/wind (Wyra). This center is about our perceptions of emotions and creativity.

The fifth belt is the "Kulli Chumpi". Its color is violet. This belt has three centers. Our right eye, "Pana Nawi", is associated with our ability to see the mystical side of the tradition and communication with the spirit-worlds. The left eye, "Lloque Nawi", is associated with the magical side of the tradition. This center is about the practical application of the Andean healing arts and the use of spiritual healing techniques and protocols. The third part of this center, the area of the brow between our two physical eyes, is the Qanchis Nawi. The third-eye is the visionary eye -the ability to see the true reality of God.

Juan has initiated many Chumpi Paqos, including Don Alberto Villoldo. For reasons unknown to me, Alberto has changed the meanings of the red and black belts and eyes (making the black connected with the realm of earth and red the realm of water).

Alberto is not trying to cheat anyone, he freely expresses that this change is a creation of his own. Does that mean that a belting ceremony with him is ineffective, or dangerous?

Of course not, Alberto is a Kurak on the Alto Misayoq path. This means his power comes from intent, and not from the correctness of his knowledge, or ritual.

Connecting to Diverse Energy Types

Part of the work on the path of a Paqo is learning to work with diverse energy types. What does this mean inside the human experience?

There are basically two qualities of inter-change in relationships. These qualities are called Yanantin and Masitin. Understanding these qualities helps us in our everyday relationships, whether they are between people, or energetic, spiritual vibrations.

Masitin is a harmonious relationship between similar energies. Masi means "equal", and tin is a suffix that means, "united together".

Yanantin is the harmonious relationships between two or more dissimilar energies. Yana means, "dark" -the opposite of light, but it also means, "boyfriend/girlfriend."

There are many dimensions and depths to Yanatin and Masitin relationships. For example, two or more men naturally fall into to a Masitin relationship.

The same is true for two or more women. The male-female pair is a natural form of Yanantin. Two people, who hold the same job, are in a Masitin relationship (no matter what their gender). Likewise, two people are in a Yanantin relationship if say, one is a law enforcement agent, and the other is part of a crime syndicate.

By examining and understanding our Masitin and Yanantin energy exchanges in our life, we can better see where Hoocha, which could lead to conflict, could arise. You also can note where similarities exist that could lead to bonding.

To truly see Masitin and Yanantin in the correct light, we add to it the understanding of complementary of opposites. For us, opposites are a needed part of each other, neither is better or worse then the other. When two opposites come into harmony, it is not through bonding on the similarities, or relating away/ homogenizing their differences. Rather, it is through bonding on our similarities, while celebrating the differences that make each a unique individual.

The Game of Relations

The Inka and the Q'ero have noted three phases of interaction: Tinkuy, Tupay, and Taqe.

Tinkuy is the first phase. It is the acknowledged meeting of another's energy. Tupay, the second phase of interaction involves sizing-up, challenging, and competing with each other. Often in the modern world, we do not get past the first or second phase. To the Q'ero, a perfect or whole interaction is one where we arrive at Taqe. Taqe is harmony between each other -realizing that the other is needed and equal to each other. I will further explain it through a metaphor:

Two runners meet each other. After sizing each other up, one challenged the other to a race. They both ran as well as they could. In the end, one wins. In the Q'ero and Andean view, the one that won has the responsibility to teach the other how he won. This is a further aspect of Taqe. Taqe is even more than this, it is a true power. It can be developed into the ability to harmonize all situations. Taqe is very powerful, and can even heal others of illnesses when developed.

Toxic People

Taqe is not an excuse for allowing others to abuse you. There are toxic people out there. These people often times are not worth conversing with. Or as Don Americo Yabar would say, "You are better off having a conversation with a flower."

How do we know if someone is toxic?

1. Toxic people will not allow you to grow beyond their image of you. They will distort anything you say or do to fit that image. They will try to mystify you from your experience. They will listen to your personal truth and try to bend it -to fit their image of you. If this does not work, they will try to alienate, negate, or excuse your experience. Toxic people also have a way of reminding you "who you are", by belittling you, and bringing up moments of your past -telling you who they need you to be.

2. Toxic people are aware of cycles of abuse in their lives and continue cycles of abuse. Often using the excuse: "it happened to me why not you?" Or, that it's, "just the way life is", or that you need "toughened up." They have a need to hold power over others, and often that power is cruelty.

3. Toxic people often are, or show signs of being a sociopath. Often they think that the world owes them something, and that they are the only person that truly matters. Some uphold a victim mentality and like to live in a co-dependent lifestyle. Any have lives involving drug abuse, or alcoholism. When someone in their community decides that they are done with the co-dependent lifestyle, the toxic people will pull out all the stops using: shame, guilt, or sympathy, to try and coax you back in.

4. Very Toxic and dangerous people, show a total disregard for the sacredness of life itself. They may torture/kill animals, rape, or murder for the rush of it. People who fit into this category are extremely rare.

Of course, those who fit into these categories are in need of help. Unfortunately, there is little one can do for them, because it involves their field of free will (if they like playing host to these energies). It does not matter what made them the way they are. They cannot be helped until they can step outside of themselves, empathize with the world, acknowledge their actions (how they have hurt those around them), and take steps to change their lives.

When you run across a person which fits into these categories, there is little you can do, except eat their Hoocha and move on. The act of eating their Hoocha, or the Hoocha Mikhuy, gives them a chance to have a mystical experience and the opportunity to empathize. The Hoocha Mikhuy will be explained in more detail, and taught later in the book.

Some people have an affinity towards toxic people. Some have a misguided need to fix toxic people. This often has to do with their lack of self-esteem and personal power. Others may have gone through hard times and personal growth themselves, and have developed compassion for toxic people. This is truly beautiful. Remember, toxic people have just as much a right to life as the rest of us. They have lessons to teach the world.

If you are in the situation where you are trying to help someone who is toxic, you have to decide what behaviors are acceptable to you and for how long. Let the person you are working with know also. Then, you must be true to yourself and not allow yourself to be abused. If the person steps over the line of what is acceptable, you must remove yourself from them. If not, you are reinforcing the very concepts that underline all toxic behaviors.

The Powers of the Unconscious

The unconscious side of us functions in the realm of the "Ukhu Pacha" -the deep underworld. It is a place of beauty, art, riches, and chaotic raw potential. This is the realm of impulse and ancestral memories. In this shadowy place, feeling is the prevalent sense. It is where the hidden and wounded selves hide from our awareness. This is the place of magic and healing.

In many new age philosophies, and self-help approaches, emotions and feelings (aside from love) are considered undesirables that are a sure sign that all self-improvement efforts have been in vain. What if this isn't true? What if feelings such as: fear, anger, jealousy, desire, pride, shame, and deception are actually necessary parts of the self.

What if I were to tell you these "feelings" are potent powers, able to bring a dramatic change to your world? So many people go through life fearing these energies, and allowing them to paralyze their actions. Many believe these feelings to be evil/negative -detracting from their quality of life.

Remember, no energy is "wrong", so don't make it so in your mind. All energies are needed and part of the whole. All have a time and place. The energies of fear, anger, and stress are meant for moments of life and death when there is no alternative but to feel this way. In a life-or-death situation, you can see how fear and anger are true powers and gifts of the universe to help us preserve life. They bring awareness and great amounts of energy to a situation that needs to be changed. Something may feel heavy, because in some way the situation at hand has broken Ayni, and is causing Hoocha to accumulate. The function of this is to bring awareness to the gravity of the situation. When we are unwilling to listen to this subtle language of energy, either because we are ashamed of feeling this way, or denying these feelings from the get-go, we effectively blind ourselves to the information stored within it. This can paralyze us from being able to understand how to remedy it. Likewise, we create (and promote) through these behaviors an idealistic standard that feeling these things is wrong/undesirable. The idea that accompanies this is that those whom feel these things are also wrong, or undesirable, as well. This leads to alienation, repression, and negation -causing a further breakdown of Ayni and a greater accumulation of heaviness.

This lesson completely hit home when I returned to the USA from living with the Q'ero. I flew into the DC airport at 3:30 pm. "Yes", I thought to myself, "plenty of time to catch my bus." Everything to this point of my return trip had gone so smoothly. By the time I finally cleared customs, it was almost 5pm. My bus was supposed to leave at 5:30pm. On my last twenty-three dollars, I frantically tried to find a ride to the station, just to find out that I did not have enough for a cab ride. Also, the bus station was at least an hour away from the airport. I realized no one could get me there in time anyway. Knowing that I had some money at home -plenty to pay for the trip, I called my best-friend Megan, only to find out her car was in the shop. I called my mother, who agreed to wire me some money, only to find out that the bank at the airport had closed. I would have to wait until the next morning before I could even arrange a wire. As a last-ditch effort, I called my other best-friend, Josh, in the hopes that his parents would let him borrow their vehicle -only to find out that it was in no shape for the trip.

Josh suggested that I try and transfer my tickets, an action I had not tried because of a bold, unfeeling, word printed on my tickets -nontransferable. Having no other options, knowing that I am going to have to spend the night at the airport, I begin to center myself. I decide to call the bus line, to find out how much I will need wired to me tomorrow. To my surprise, I found out my tickets were transferable for a fifteen-dollar charge. I only had to make it to the bus station by 5:45 am, or I would have to wait until 5:45 am the next morning. I decided I had the time to at least walk to the bus station. I found out I could ride a city bus, catch a couple metro subways, and make it within a couple blocks of the station.

On the bus and subway rides, everyone I met was so helpful and nice. It amazed me to find the same open-hearted kindness I had found in Peru in the subways of Washington DC. I arrived at a little after 10 pm at the bus station, and thanked the Apus for such a wonderful lesson. I sat and chit-chatted with those around me, having a very enjoyable time.

At around 12:30 am, a bus pulled up. As the people entered the station, you could literally feel the energy change. I thought only I had noticed, but realized that everyone in the station had stopped talking. The people from the bus had an air of hardness about them and did not speak to each other. Most of the passengers wore dated clothes that were in remarkably good shape. They placed themselves around the station, standing in front of the doors. They sat down on both sides of me. Figuring all of this tension was being caused by heard mentality, I centered myself, and I asked the person that was sitting closest to me how long they were laid-over for. The response, I never could have imagined. He and two of his cohorts, turned, and began staring at me with a squinted-eyed death look, like some demented episode of the three stooges. They continued to stare like this at me, without saying a word for the next 10 minutes, before finally turning their heads away.

Being the poor son of a Baptist preacher, I have sat and talked to gangsters, murders, thieves, and drug dealers. During my apprenticeship as a Catholic Funeral Director, I had met, talked with, and gotten to know, true old-school Mafioso's. In my youth, I had followed the dead, and was a part of the alternative culture. I had never, in my collected experience, encountered anything like this. About every 15 minutes or so, one or more of the group sitting beside me, would turn and give me the evil eye. Refusing to be intimidated, I sat there harmonizing with their energy and group bubble. I even went to sleep two or three times. Each time I woke up, I could see they were more aggravated. It went on like this for the next two hours. The last time I opened my eyes, I realized all of the others had fled.

Reading their energy, I realized they did not look for comfort in themselves, but through outward intimidation, confrontation and dominance. They had to establish a pecking order. I realized, or read off of them, that they had been in prison and were still feeling like trapped animals. Only one (out of about 20 people) had socks. As I read their energy, I started to feel fear. The fear made me alert; I had noticed off-and-on, how they were staring at my luggage bag, especially one guy. I noticed he was looking at the Columbia tag from my connecting flight. I felt his energy become more and more nervous; he physically started sweating.

Feeling his thoughts, I heard him telling himself, "no", not to do it. I realized, I was about to be mugged, if not by him, then one of his cohorts. I also realized, that my general comfort and ease, had kept it from happening until that moment. They had never experienced anything like it before, and figured I must be connected -to be so at ease around them. This uncertainty was now wearing off, and they were getting ready to act. Listening to my fear, I calmly stood up and slowly made my way to the restaurant at the other end of the station. Soon, I saw that this was the idea all of the people I was chatting with before the bus arrived. We sat there in the heightened awareness of fear for the next hour, until they were forced by a police officer to board their bus.

After putting all the pieces together, the dated clothes, no socks, and the odd behavior, and my intuitions, I think that they were a bus of newly released convicts. Upon release, they were probably given a bus ticket. I know this is a common practice. I still honor these men. Who knows how I would have behaved, had I lived their experiences of life? These men were just acting out of their truth of life. This was definitely the right time and place for fear.

Hoocha Mikhuy

"Mikhuy", means to digest, transform, and change. When one eats food, it starts a process of breaking down and transforming the food into usable substances for the body.

Pachamama, our mother, has the ability to digest all forms of living energy in the universe. She transforms all of this energy into raw, chaotic, creative potential -a kind of super refined black Sami we call, "Wilka" which means, "sacred and dangerous." This powerful energy can be used for any purpose. Humans have group memories of times in our history that we used this energy to exert power over others.

The art of Mikhuy can be subtle, yet powerful, when mastered.

To perform the Hoocha Mikhuy, we start with the opening the Qosqo exercise from chapter 7. However, this time we extend the Qosqo until it is at complete arms length. At this time, your Qosqo is connected to your bubble. All you have to do, is intend to pull in the Hoocha into your Qosqo nawi and intend to digest the Hoocha. When you start digesting it will be obvious, because you will feel a split-stream of energy (one rising up from the Nawi, the other flowing down from the Nawi).

Mastering the Mikhuy

Mastering the Hoocha Mikhuy is accomplished in several stages. The first is accomplished by eating your own Hoocha. The second process involves eating the Hoocha of a close friend. The third exercise is eating the Hoocha of someone you don't know, and the last is eating the Hoocha of your greatest enemy. At this point, you are ready to use the Hoocha Mikhuy for healing.

I tell my students (for the third stage) to pick the longest line at a store, and choose the person that is having the toughest time being in the line to perform the digestion on.

At this point during live teachings, I am often asked about ethics. Some feel it is unethical to take Hoocha from someone without their permission. Others bring up the point: if we are the masters of our bubble, and nothing comes in, or goes out, without our permission −then how is it possible to eat a person's Hoocha without their permission?

Both of these questions have the same answer. It is absolutely true that you are the master of your bubble; nothing comes in, or goes out, without your permission. The thing about Hoocha is: that humans are always trying to rid themselves of it. For example, the person in the long store line: their body language, heavy sighs, impatient movements, etc... are all ways they are releasing the heaviness they are feeling. Sigmund Freud called it the pleasure principal; in the end we (humans) are always trying to re-establish well-being.

Hapu the Sacred Couple

Hapu, is the sacred couple symbolizing the finest form of a Yanantin relationship. It is the perfect, harmonized unity of two dissimilar energies. This happens when a Yanantin pair (opposing energies) starts to compliment each other -synergistically helping each other to grow and develop. This is seen in the same way that limestone activates coca, or sugar sweetens tea. Hapu, is an important part in our spiritual development as well.

This stage of our development comes with the realization that within each of us, is a part of the other sex. For example: I, as a man, have healed my inner-masculinity, and realize that I have an inner-feminine side. Since I am a man, I do not have the ability, or understandings, to heal and tame my feminine side. I cannot do this for myself. For this, I must take a woman as my master, learning about my feminine-side from her. At the same time, I am teaching her about her inner-masculine side. The end result is: the forming of the Hapu, or divine couple, inside of each of us.

The Ch'aska

Walking with the Kuraq, Don Marcos, to his home on the outskirts of the Q'ero village of Kiko, we were discussing, in-depth, the work of the Kuraq. Don Marcos said to me, "We work with Pachamama, Inti Tayta, Wyra Nusta, Apu but most importantly, we work with the "Ch'aska" -the stars. I did not tell him, but I had just found my star a year before. It had become the focus of my work since.

The star is the purest light of our true-self; it comes to a Paqo when he/she learns to attain a subconscious silence. This takes many years, even a lifetime to accomplish. It is achieved by working through/eradicating personal fears and fear-based behavior. This is done by pushing our boundaries of self out into the stars. When we find our star, we find our last great teacher. In our star is our higher genius.

Once a Kurak attains such a state, they seem to radiate a peace and calm to all that come within their presence.

The Kutichi Ceremony

The Kutichi is a ceremony for reconnecting with your essential self, by yourself. Puma talks about being at the center of your own web, and not letting your connections to others pull you off center. This ceremony is one way to keep centered in our personal power.

It is a very simple ceremony. It is not about how you do it, but what your intent is, and what quality of energy you bring to your undertaking. It is a ceremony where you reintroduce yourself to yourself, and detach from everything -so that you can perceive your own essence. We get pulled out of our essence by cords connected from the past and insecurities. In this ceremony, you detach all the seqes, or energy cords, that connect you with others. After doing this, you are "purely you" and in a state of stillness. To do this, you sit comfortably, cleanse your bubble using Saminchukuy, and release all your connections to everyone in your present and past. You literally unhook yourself from everybody and everything you have been in relationships with. Don't try re-living your life emotionally, or even visually. You stay detached, but aware on an energy level, and perceive the Seqe coming into your poq'po (bubble) and cutting them. You can feed the energy to Pachamama, or into water. As you do this, you will begin to get more and more in touch with your "salka", or your undomesticated, unrefined energies.

When you feel content, prepare a Kutichi Despacho. It is a simple Despacho. You offer a shell on white paper. Then, make four kintu's to place around the shell. Sometimes, the kintus are offered counterclockwise, to symbolize ancient memories, instead of clockwise. Trust your intuition when deciding how to offer your kintu to the Apus.

Fold the Despacho, and tie it with white string (cotton or natural fiber). Unhook any seqe that you notice are still attached, and cleanse any Hoocha from your bubble with the Despacho. Offer the Despacho to the spirits of nature (again, sometimes this is done to the 4 or 6 directions in a counterclockwise direction).

Build a small fire and offer the Despacho. As you watch the Despacho burn, unhook any other cords that might still be in your bubble. Stay in a meditative state, allowing yourself to perceive yourself purely: the original you with no projections from others or self. Once the Despacho is fully burned, the ceremony ends. Soon you will start to be connected to Seqes. Again, the first ones are connections from love. All people, places, and things we are connected to through love reconnect as soon as the ceremony ends. Any cords that were only giving Hoocha, will not reconnect. While alone with your fundamental self, you are given an opportunity to sense who you are, what you desire, how you want to be, and so on. This rite is done at least once a year.

The Lloque

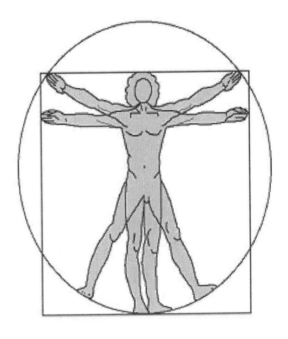

The Lloque is the magical side it has to do with developing your ability to act. It is the functional application of mystical wisdom for remedies healing and self development. Here we work from the skin of the bubble inwards learning to express our innate qualities to the world.

Chapter 8

Karpay through Life Experience

Stepping into Your Becoming

The word "Karpay", means, "initiation", or transmission. There are many types of transmissions in the life of a Paqo. All people naturally receive important insights or knowledge from events in their earth-walk. These events often change us and the course of our lives.

One of the major life Karpays I went through was a bad car wreck that left me in a three-day coma. During this time, I had an amazing experience of meeting/talking with my grandmother. We met under a rainbow. Before I woke, my grandma told me it was our rainbow, and that we could always meet there. She told me to ask her about it the next time talked in day-today life. When I asked her, she smiled, and said, the same words: "That is our rainbow. We will always be able to find each other no matter how we are separated. Even in death, we can meet there." This was a very powerful reinforcement for my experience. Because of this, and other things I experienced from that car wreck, I decided I had to follow my dreams -my heart-path.

A few years later, I was returning from working with Juan in Vermont (and a 12-hour car ride home). When we pulled into the house, my Mom was waiting for me. She ran up and told me, "Grandmother is in the hospital with congestive heart-failure. I fear it's pretty bad, and she might not make it." I rushed to the hospital to be with her. My friends told me later, they were asking my grandmother's spirit to let me work with her.

In the hospital room, I started talking to her. She looked so gray. She told me, "I think I'm going to die". I held her hand and asked, "Grandma, do you mind if I lay hands on you?" She said, "Do you believe in what you are doing?" I told her, with confidence, "Yes". With that, she agreed. I told her, "All that fear you feel, all that pain and heaviness -just give it to me. Just imagine you are giving it to me. Don't be worried, I know what to do with it". At this point, I began the Hoocha Mikhuy. My grandma was a type of Christian mystic. So, I called out to help in her healing, "Gabriel, Michael, Sachiel, Uriel". To my amazement, the room grew dark. Strange shadows were moving everywhere. I felt a soft squeeze, like time was collapsing in on us. It felt to me like we were always here, living in this moment, like our whole lives had been crafted for this one event. I could see in the four corners of the room, massive pillar-like beings -the angels I assumed. They seemed to swallow the light in the room as it came close to them. At that moment, my grandmother grabbed my hand tightly and started to convulse. Twisting and squirming, holding my hand tighter, she looked up at me with tears in her eyes, pleading. She started confessing her sins and the things she was ashamed of to me. It came in waves. Her muscles would tighten up. She would start shaking and confessing, as another wave of encrusted Hoocha would break free. I literally could see a black, oily fluid come rushing out of her eyes and mouth, like a spiritual purge. Then, it would seem, the wave and internal pressure would subside for a moment. It went on like this for about a half an hour.

As horrific as this may sound, I felt completely detached from it. As wave after wave hit I started to hear murmuring like a dozen voices talking. I could hear a mocking laughter. I was eating as much of this oil-like Hoocha that I could. The rest of it would flow onto the floor, where it seemed to be sucked into the four angels. The angels looked as though they were pillars made of this same substance. Soon, the strange noises stopped. The shadows subsided. Grandmother relaxed as the angels dissolved into the shadows, and light returned to the room. Everything felt open and clear -like a beautiful dawn on a spring morning. I swiped her arms and legs with my mesa, removing the last bits of Hoocha. As I looked down, I noticed the color had returned to her. The desperation I had felt in her was gone. She returned home, living another two years in great health, until she passed away at the ripe old age of 94.

After I left the hospital, I visited another acquaintance and ran into someone that had recently stolen money from me. He was standing against the wall, holding his arm. He nervously said, "I'm sorry, man." I said, "Don't worry about it. What's up with your arm?" It looked strangely angled and was purple and splotchy. He said, "I was wrestling with my brother". "My arm got pinned and popped out of place. Now I can barely move it at all".

I told him I was a healer and asked if I could work on it he replied, "Sure." I Preformed the Phukuy and called my helpers. I stepped into his bubble, cupping his shoulder in my hand. I could feel the soft relaxation of Sami flowing through me. There were no angels or fantastic visuals, like with my grandmother's healing just an hour ago. When the flux of energy subsided, I waved my mesa around the shoulder and told him he should feel better soon. He thanked me and walked to his car to leave. As he was pulling away from the place, he honked, raised his hurt arm and waved goodbye. The look of shock on his face was evident.

The Cardinal

One day my friends Josh, Megan, and I, were sitting in the living room, when we heard a crash on the window behind us. I looked out and didn't see anything so I ran out to investigate. At the bottom of the stairs, was a baby cardinal just old enough that it had started to turn its tell-tail crimson. I poked it up in my hands it wasn't breathing. Josh and Megan rushed down to see what I had. You could clearly see it had a broken neck. The bones weren't jutting out, but you could see both sides of the fracture pushing against its skin. I closed my eyes and preformed Phukuy through the bird, calling the nature beings to help. Josh and Megan, also being healers, reached out their hands and started to flow energy. I reached out my Qosqo, swallowed the bird's energy, and took its spirit to the upper-world. I laid the bird at Wiraqocha creator's feet, and said, "You can stay here or return with me" -at that moment, the cardinal flipped over in my hand and spread out its wings. It sat there, in my cupped hands, wings out-stretched rolling its head back and forth. It then flew from my hands to my tomato patch close by. From the patch, it flew to join the other birds. This was one of the most amazing spiritual experiences in my life. For the first few years after that, I always thought that I took the bird's spirit to the upper-world and creator. I now feel, perhaps, it was the bird's spirit that took me on its journey to the creator. All I did was make known the option that it could return and held open the gate.

Story of James

Juan told me to work with the terminally ill. This turned out to be harder then I thought. Many terminal folk just don't care anymore; many want to die. Then one day, out of the blue, a friend of mine stopped by to see me. I wasn't home but he had stopped to say goodbye. He stopped by a few days latter, his voice was almost gone he looked gray. He told me his esophagus was mostly dissolved, he had a hole in his heart and three shadows on his lungs. The culprit was crack cocaine. He said he was given a month to live. I asked if he minded if I worked with him -he said, "Please do." So, I arranged a time for the next week to meet with him and perform a healing. The day arrived I was very nervous about what to do. I mean, this guy is dying; he has given up hope. This was one of those moments where you push through with courage. Courage gives you the ability to act in the face of insurmountable odds.

We begin our session. I preformed Phukuy, asked my helpers, Apus, and local nature beings to help. Standing, facing each other, I put my hands on his head and joined with his bubble. I opened a Saminchukuy through us (When you join bubbles with something the group Hoocha is felt and worked with as you would personal Hoocha). I allowed the Saminchukuy to flux and end naturally. I then moved my mesa to his navel. I told him to give me all that is heavy and bothering him to me. I told him to imagine he is giving it to me through his navel, as a great gift. I began Hoocha Mikhuy. He started to shake; we both started to sweat. I continued until I felt such strange sensations in my head that I could barley stand. A few minuets later, he told me that it was the strangest thing he ever felt; he told me he could feel himself draining through the navel. I taught him to perform the Saminchukuy for himself. We made plans to meet again the next week. We met three times after that occasion. To make a long story short, Jim is now happily married and has been healthy for over seven years.

Chapter 9

Dream-Weaving

Dream-weaving is also referred to as: "Dreaming Your World into Being".

How is this done?

Well, throughout our work on this path, or any spiritual path, we become acquainted with the energies of the living universe, Kausay Pacha. As we use the toys of the tradition to play with our reality, we have found that we are in constant relationships with the entire universe. As we work to understand the Yanatin and Masitin relationships in our lives, we improve the quality of our energetic exchanges with others, nature beings and the spiritual world. This has made Sami, or refined energies, that lead to relaxation and well-being becoming our predominate energy. As we taste and learn to accept more flavors of the Kausay Pacha, we learn to see more of the reality around us. We are pushing our limits, thus, stretching the bubble to blend and harmonize with more of reality. As stated in chapter two, our bubble is completely ours; you are in charge of your bubble. As our bubble increases, so does the influence of our sacred space.

The true art of dream-weaving is beyond our ideas of mystical or magical arts. It is about walking in the flow of life in such a close relationship with it, you can anticipate its moves, and it anticipates yours. It is a type of co-operative synchronicity.

Biography

Zane Curfman is an initiated Kurak Akulleq (fourth level shaman/priest). He is a healer, and teacher of the Andean spiritual path. Zane created the Salka Munay Ayllu: a religious organization that puts on workshops and events based around the Andean spiritual and healing arts. 10% of the proceeds of all Ayllu events go to the Q'ero Indians of Peru.

In 2009, Zane traveled to the Q'ero nations. There he was honored as an elder of the tradition. He was made a part of the Q'ero nation of Kiko. He has been asked to be a Chacana (bridge between cultures).

For more info please visit the Ayllu: www.SalkaMunay.com

Glossary

Alto Misayoq (alto-meez-eye-yoke) High Priest. An Andean Priest of the third level.

Apu (Ah-pooh) Lord. Mountain spirit. The tutelary nature deity of a village or region, inhabiting the peaks of the highest Mountain. Classically there are twelve tutelary mountain spirits of Cuzco city: APU AUSANGATE, APU SALKANTAY, MAMA SIMONA, APU PIKOL, APU MANUEL PINTA, APU WANAKAURI, APU PACHATUSAN, APU PIJCHU, APU SAQSAYWAMAN, APU WIRAQOCHAN, APU PUKIN, APU SENQ'A. Apus are generally male nature energies, except for a few aberrant females like Mama Simona in Cuzco, Veronica in the Sacred Valley, and Putukusi in Machu Pijchu.

Atawalpa (ah-ta-wal-pah) twelfth ruler of the Inka Culture. Son of Wayna Qapaq and his Equadorian Queen. He waged war against his brother half brother,Waskar, and lost his ruling power. Because he and Waskar inherited the Inka culture and did not return one to their children, they broke the law of ayni, therefore becoming full of heavy energy and sinking to the underworld. Myth states that he and Waskar are in the underworld now teaching ayni to the beings there until they can return to this world.

Ayllu (eye-lyoo) family and/or spiritual community to which one belongs.

Ayllu Apu (eye-lyu ah-pooh) A local tutelary mountain spirit who oversees a small village or community, related with the first level of the Andean path.

Ayni (eye-nee) Sacred reciprocity. If you give you will receive and if you receive you must give back. This is the one law of the Andean Mystical Tradition still often witnessed in small mountain villages today. A way of life founded by the Inkas upon which, in the high Andes, one's very survival depends.

Chumpi (Choom-peeh) Belt. In Andean mysticism this term also refers to the belts of living energy that surround the human body and make up the human 'bubble' or energy field.

Chumpi Paqo In Andean Mysticism this refers to a special designation of mystical priest initiated in the art of the chumpi's, or, opening the energy belts.

Ch'uncho (choon-cho) A traditional hourglass design in Q'ero weaving, it is a symbol of the jungle dancer.

Despacho (des-pah-cho) A Spanish word popularly used to refer to the traditional Andean offering of thanks or supplication sent to the Nature Spirits. Despachos can contain up to 200 different ingredients and are made in a ceremony performed by Andean Priests. This offering is traditionally burned, buried, or sunk in a lake or other body of water depending on the meaning and purpose of the offering. HAYWARISQA is the actual quecua term.

Hanpiq (hom-pek) To cure.

Hanpiq Runa (hom-pek roo-nah) Curandero. Healer.

Hanpuy (hon-pwee) Command form of the verb to come used by Andean Priests to call the spirit of a person, god, teacher, or a nature being. COME!

Hanak Pacha (hah-nak pah-cha) The upper or superior world, defined by it's abundance of super-refined energy or *sami*.

Hapu (ha-pooh) SACRED COUPLE-finest form of Yanantin. A sacred couple who have both reached full development of the three human powers: mind, heart, and body.

Hatun (Hah-toon) Great, big, or high. See Hatun Karapy and/or Hatun Q'eros.

Hatun Karpay (hah-toon kar-pie) The Great or High Initiation or Transmission.**Hatun Q'eros** (hah-toon keros) High Q'eros. This town serves as the ceremonial center, umbilicus or Qosqo of the Q'ero Nation.

Haywarisqa (Hi-wa-ree-ska) traditional Andean offering to the Gods, Despacho.

Hoocha (hoo-chah) Heavy energy. Mistranslated by the Spanish as "sin."

Hoocha Mikhuy (hoo-chah meekh-hwee) To eat and digest heavy energy with the Qosqo.

Inka (in-kah) a ruling class of people inhabiting the Cuzco valley in the late 1100's to 1532 A. D. Possibly comes from ancient word *enqa* which means "black hole" or one who can absorb all the living energies.

Inka Mallku (in-kah mal-koo) A male initiate of the fifth-level. One who can heal every illness, every time, with only a single touch. The female counterpart is **Nust'a.**
Mallku comes from the root word meaning tree, thus Inka Mallky also means "one connected to the spiritual geneaology of the Inkas."

Inti (in-tee) The living being we call the Sun.

Inti Tayta (in-teeh ti-tah) Father Sun.

Itu Apu (eeh-too ah-pooh) masculine spirit of one's place of birth, also known as the "guiding star."

K'intu (keen-too) Sacred coca leaves, generally a bundle of three perfect coca leaves, chosen as an offering to the Nature Spirits. K'intu are generally used in multiples of three when making despachos.

Kamasqa (kah-mas-kah) Unique type of fourth-level priest who receives *kurak akulleq* initiation (fourth level) directly from God or Wiraqocha.

Karpay (kar-pie) Initiation or Transmission. See Hatun Karpay.

Kausay (cowz-eye) Living energy.

Kausay Pacha (cowz-eye pah-chah) The world of living energies. The energy universe.

Kausay Poq'po (cowz-eye poke-poh) The bubble of living energy around a human, plant, animal, town, mountain, or nature being.

Kay Pacha (kai pah-cha) The world of material consciousness. The "middle" world, filled with both heavy and refined living energies, typically symbolized by the Puma.

Khuya (koo-yah) impassioned love.

Khuya Rumi (koo-yah roo-mee) gift stone of teacher to disciple.

K'intu (k' een- tooh) a bundle of three perfect coca leaves used to make an offering to the Nature Spirits. K'intu are a central element in the despacho and are generally used in multiples of three.

Kurak Akulleq (koo-rock akool-yek) Great chewer of coca leaves, this term refers to a fourth-level priest.Llanqay (lyon-kai) The power of the body, industriousness. The power of physical work.

Llaqta Apu (lyak-tah ah-pooh) This is a medium-sized tutelary Mountain Spirit related with the second level of the Andean Path.

Lloque (Lyo-kay) Left-hand side of the path. Relates to the magical knowledge or application of spiritual knowledge in the physical world. Healing, magic, therapy, remedies, all are considered gifts of the left-hand side of the path. The complement is pana, or right–hand knowledge (see pana).

Mama Qocha (Mama-ko-chah) Female spirit of the great ocean, water,
mother of all waters.

Masintin (mahs-een-teen) Harmonious relationship between similar things, homolgous.

Masy (mass-eeh) Equal.

Masychakuy (mah-sa-cha-kwee) The act of joining two similar energy bubbles. (See Yanachakuy)

Mesa (may-suh) A Spanish word signifying the collection of *khuyas* or power objects given by the teacher or Nature Spirits to the *paqo* (initiate). The mesa is a physical extension of the Andean Priests power and is used in almost all ceremonies.

Mikhuy (meekh-wee) To eat and digest living energy. Hoocha Mikhuy is the practice of eating and digesting heavy energy.

Muju (Moo-hoo) Seed. Can be a literal seed for planting, or the spiritual seed within each person. The Hatun Karpay provides the living energy necessary to germinate the seed.

Mullu Khuya (mool-yoo koo-yah) A specific set of five stones, progressively carved with one to five humps, used to open the human energy belts. These are the tools of the chumpi paqo.

Munay (Moo-nai) The power of love and will together.

Nust'a (nyu-stah) Female nature spirit, Inka princess, female of 5th level.

Pachakuti (pah-cha-koo-tee) literally world turned upside down. In Inka history this terms refers to a cosmic transmutation occuring between one era and the next.

Pachakuteq (pah-cha koo-tek) Ninth Inka Ruler attributed with building most of the Inka Culture.

Pachakamaq (pa-cha-ka-mak) Creator. He who puts order in the world. A temple outside of Lima where the philosophy of *yanantin* was born.

Pachamama (pa-cha-mah-mah) Mother Earth.

Pampa Misayoq (pahm-pah mee-sigh-yoke) An Andean priest who specializes in rituals like performing despachos or coca leaf readings.

Panaka (pah-nah-kah) In Inka times this word refers to the twelve royal lineages of Inka families that competed in Wiraqocha Temple to become the next Sapa Inka or ruler of the Culture.

Paqarina (pah-ka-ree-nah) female nature spirit who is the guardian of one's birthplace. Most prominent feminine aspect of the natural geography at one's birth site. Female counterpart of the *Itu Apu.*

Paqo (pah-ko) Initiate or student of the Andean Path.

Pana (pa-nya) right handside of the path, relating to mystical knowledge. The cold, rational, objective and structured side of the path governing initiation and ritual. Known as "the road to God."

Phausi Runa (pow-see roo-nah) Little nature deities inhabiting running water: streams, creeks, and waterfalls.

Phutuy (pooh-tooh-ee) Flowering of a plant or of the spiritual seed of the initiate.

Poq'po (poke-poh) Literally means "bubble" and refers to the field of living energy surrounding the human body.

Pukllay (poohk-ly-eye) The play of children, lovers, or the playing out of a ritual.

Putukusi (pooh-tooh-kooh-see) The name of the female mountain just at the entrance to the ruins of Machu Pijchu. Her name means "Flowering Joy."

Qawaq (cow-wak) Clairvoyant, or "seer of living energy."

Qayqa (kay-kah) A psychic or energetic knot of energy released through healing, ritual or intiation work, often causing the initiate or patient to choke or dry heave.

Qollana (koy-ya-na) Excellence. In mystical training this refers to the student who keeps the teacher honest by continually pointing out inconsistencies or contradictions in their teaching. Teacher's Pet Inka style!

Qorimoqo (ko-ree-mo-koh) Golden Mountain. This is the Apu that watches over Hatun Q'eros.

Q'ollorit'i (kol-yo-ree-tee) An ancient festival in the high Andes attended by more than eighty-thousand indigenous people. Literally the word means "white as snow," or "purity."

Qosqo (kos-koh) Spiritual Stomach. Also, the ancient name for the Inka capital, meaning "navel of the world." In mystical terms *qosqo* refers to the energy center located near the physical navel. It's function is to eat and digest living energy.

Qoya (koy-yah) Queen. Female or Priestess of the sixth level.

Killa (keel-yah) Moon, or the female living energy or consciousness of the moon, oftened referred to as Mama killya, Mother Moon.

Ranti (ran-teeh) Equivalent.

Rumi (roo-mee) Stone.

Runa (roo-nah) Man, human, or being.

Runa Simi (rooh-nah see-mee) The tongue of man, the language of the Inkas.

Saiwa (sigh-wah) A tall column of stones built by an Andean Priest to represent his/her power, or a column of living energy.

Sami (sah-mee) refined energy.

Sapa (Sah-pah) Unique, the one and only.

Sapa Inka (sah-pah een-kah) The Inka ruler.

Seqe (say-kay) Line of living energy running through the earth, or between two ritual sites.

Seqe Rumi (say-kay room-ee) Stone of living energy lines. A sacred shrine in Hatun Q'eros.

Simi (see-mee) Tongue or language.

Sinak'ara (see-nah-ke-ara) The overlighting mountain deity of the Q'ollorit'i Festival.

Soq'a (sohk-hah) Twisted female nature spirit. More accurately, a third level initiates vision of a powerful female nature spirit. When fear is conquered, the frightening Soq'a transforms into a beautiful Nust'a.

Suyu Apu (soo-yoo ah-pooh) A large-sized tutelary Mountain Spirit overseeing an entire region, related with the third level of the Andean Path.

Taki Ongoy (tah-kee on-goy) Collective delirium brought about by singing. In Inka history the Taki Ongoy refers to the National Inka Movement of the 1700's that nearly overthrew the Spanish.

Taripaypacha (tah-ree-pie-pah-cha) Literally meaning "encounter with the universe," in Andean Prophecy this word refers to a new golden era in the human experience. It is known as the "age of meeting ourselves again"—and heralds coming together again of the Andean people, and the recreation of a new and better Inka Culture.

Taytacha (tie-tah-cha) Father, Lord.

Taytacha Temblores (tie-tah-cha tem-blo-rayz) Lord of the Earthquakes. This refers to an icon (statue) of the black Christ given to the city of Cuzco by Charles the fifth of Spain. It was paraded around Cuzco during a terrible earthquake and is considered by the people to have the power to stop earthquakes. This is a powerful guiding star for many Andean Priests.

Taytanchis Ranti (tie-than-chees rahn-tee) Equivalent to God on Earth. This term refers to the powers and capacity of the seventh level initiate in the Andean system of psychospiritual development. According to Inka prophecy the seventh level priest will be capable of ressurecting their own physical bodies after death.

Tawantin (tah-wahn-teen) Four united together.

Tawantinsuyu (tah-wahn-tin soo-yoo) Four corners, or four regions. The ancient quechua name of the Inka Culture.

Taqe (tah-kay) To join forces, or join energy bubbles. To bring together in harmony.

Tinkuy (teen-kwee) Encounter, meeting.

Tukuy (too-kwee) Complete, fully developed.

Tukuymunayniyoq (too-kwee-moo-nie-nee-yoke) The fully developed power of the heart.

Tukuyyachayniyoq (too-kwee-ya-chai-nee-yoke) The fully developed power of the mind.

Tukuyllanqayniyoq (too-kwee-lyonk-eye-nee-yoke) The fully developed power of the body.

Tukuy Hanpiq (too-kwee hon-peek) The fully developed or complete healing power. Refers to the fifth level of psycho-spiritual development and the healing abilities of the Inka Mallku.

Tupay (too-pie) Conflict. Spiritual sparring of two Andean priests.

Tupaq (too-pok) Challenge. As a title "One who challenges."

Ukhu Pacha (oohk-hoo pah-cha) Interior world, lower world, underworld, unconscious, or inside of the planet. The world within, traditionally symbolized by the serpent.

Unu Kausay (ooh-noo cowz-eye) The living energy of water. Water spirit.

Wacho (wah-cho) Lineage. Row of earth dug to plant seeds. The waking spiritual seed in people.

Waka (wah-kah) Sacred. Often spelled "huaca" this also refers to any sacred object or place of the Inkas.

Waskar (wah-skar) The son of Huayna Qapaq and the last "officially selected" ruler of the Inka Culture.

Wanu (wah-noo) Death, or life after life.

Wayra Kausay (why-rha cowz-eye) The living energy or spirit of the wind.

Winay (win-yay) Germination. Again this refers to plant germination as well as the spiritual germination of the initiates "seed."

Willka (veel-kah) Sacred and dangerous.

Willka Nust'a (veel-kah nyoo-stah) Princess of the black light. Ancient name of the Urubamba River.

Wiraqocha (wee-rah-ko-cha) Lord. God. Creator. Title of respect. The Q'ero use this term to refer to one another meaning something like "good sir."

Yachay (yah-chai) The power of the mind.

Yanachakuy (yah-nah-cha-kwee) The Andean ritual for joining together two different energy bubbles.

Yanantin (Yah-nahn-teen) harmonious relationship between different things. What we usually conceive as opposites the Inkas conceive as complements, i.e., male and female, light and dark, right and left.

Made in the USA
Middletown, DE
01 September 2016